SUISEKI

Classic Japanese Stone Gardening

WILLI BENZ

水石

Sterling Publishing Co., Inc.
New York

Library of Congress Cataloging-in-Publication Data

Benz, Willi
    [Suiseki, English]
    The art of Suiseki : classic Japanese stone gardening / Willi Benz.
        p.   cm.
    Includes index.
    ISBN 0-8069-6315-8
    1. Suiseki. I. Title.
NK8715.B4613 1999
745.58'4—dc21   98-53453
                                                                  CIP

1 3 5 7 9 10 8 6 4 2

Published by Sterling Publishing Company, Inc.
387 Park Avenue South, New York, N.Y. 10016
Originally published and copyright © in Germany under the title
Suiseki: Kunstwerke der Natur Präsentiert von Menschen
by Verlag Bonsai-Centrum Heidelberg
English adaptation © 1996 by Jean Michel Guillaumond
Distributed in Canada by Sterling Publishing
℅Canadian Manda Group, One Atlantic Avenue, Suite 105
Toronto, Ontario, Canada M6K 3E7
Distributed in Great Britain and Europe by Cassell PLC
Wellington House, 125 Strand, London WC2R 0BB, England
Distributed in Australia by Capricorn Link (Australia) Pty Ltd.
P.O. Box 6651, Baulkham Hills, Business Centre, NSW 2153, Australia
Printed in Hong Kong
All rights reserved

Sterling ISBN 0-8069-6315-8

Contents

Foreword

Since man began walking on this earth, he has noticed odd-looking stones that have been shaped by nature over a period of thousands of years. Some people thought the stones were miracles of the Creation. Others felt the need to adorn themselves with them. A number of people believed that, because of their hardness and durability, stones convey magical powers. These people still use stones for rituals, as is the case with the *mani* stones in Nepal, for instance.

Suiseki are natural works of art made of stone. Various forces create them, and they possess a strong radiating and suggestive power. Indeed, the most significant feature of these stones is their capacity to move the observer. The viewer often feels connected to a unique natural scene or an outstanding work of art. This radiating power is the result of a unique combination of proportion, texture, and color. The owner of such a stone expresses himself in a very personal and original way by placing it in a *suiban,* for example.

The characteristics of a stone may not be immediately obvious. Its emanating power is only expressed with an appropriate display, for example, in determining precisely its front and in choosing an appropriate *daiza* or *suiban.*

The intuition of a creative person transforms the stone into a work of art, disclosing the being of the stone and turning it into a meaningful suiseki.

This process can take a long time. I have approached the art of suiseki with commitment, without knowing which works of art nature has preserved for us. However, studying the people of the Far East and their culture has opened my eyes to the beauties of nature. An old Chinese proverb says, "Nature reveals its wonders only to the one who keeps bonsai and suiseki in his heart."

The objective of this book is to help you enter this wonderful world of nature. Works of art created by nature are for everyone and should be accessible to everyone.

Now, I would like to thank all my suiseki friends who, by exchanging ideas on the subject, contributed to this work.

Particularly, I wish to mention my Chinese, Indonesian, Japanese, Korean, and European friends who allowed me to use photographs of their stones.

Last but not least, I would like to thank all the employees of the publishing house, Mr. Klaus Zimmer for the exact page setting, and my wife. They all contributed to the realization of this book.

Willi Benz, Ketsch 1995
President of the German Suiseki Society
Vice President of the European Suiseki Association
Honorary Counsellor of the Bonsai Club of Germany

Looking through the opening in this suiseki, we can see endlessly into the distance. Lost in thought, we enter the wonderful world of suiseki. (Collection of M. Paiman, Jakarta.)

Preface by M. Paiman

The *aisek*, or "beloved stone," has the same meaning in Chinese, Japanese, and Korean. The word comes from the Kanji words *ai*, "beloved," and *sek*, "stone." These natural creations are highly valued. The Japanese call this art form *suiseki*, the Koreans call it *susok*, and the Chinese call it *shang-sek* or *yah-sek*. *Aisek* originated in ancient China. After considerable effort by contemporary Asian enthusiasts, it is now an acknowledged art form specific to that region.

As a result of the rapid changes taking place within global culture, suiseki has received both attention and recognition from the West, and a culture of stone appreciation is emerging. In each place where it takes root, it is shaped by different social and cultural factors and by the geographical features of the environment that affect any description of *aisek*, its meaning, and its beauty.

Because of the many international meetings, exhibitions, seminars, and discussions, enthusiasts from all over the world have been able to meet each other and to deepen their understanding of the "art stone." They have learned to appreciate the timeless beauty of the exterior of the stone, with all its artistic values, and the internal beauty which arises from the spiritual meaning of each stone as it interacts with the beholder.

A broader understanding of suiseki and a commitment to the international movement have produced a more cohesive flow of information. In this way, what was once a traditional art form is developing on the international level as a contemporary movement.

The growth of this "art stone" movement helps nurture and sensitize the soul of the individual, which has a positive effect on society in general. Developments in trade and technology occur so rapidly that they often produce negative effects on individuals and on society. Stress, aggression, and the destruction of the environment are all examples of societal problems caused by technology. The spirit of *aisek* promotes both a love of nature and a love of mankind.

Mr. Wilhelm Benz has been active in promoting the art of bonsai and *aisek*. With hard work and persistence, he has gathered information and knowledge about the art of the stone. This has been a challenging task, considering the difficulty in accessing data in East Asian countries.

In these few words of introduction, I would like to express my appreciation of the dedication and high aspirations with which Wilhelm has made this book. Just like the *aisek*, it has been shaped by years of struggle and by many influences. Now it has achieved a meaning and a life of its own. It is my sincere hope that this book will stimulate further interest and a wider realization of the potential role of *aisek* in beautifying human existence.

M. Paiman
Vice President
International Natural Artistic Stone Association
Chairman of the Indonesian Suiseki Association

Introduction

As the president of the European Suiseki Association (ESA), a European organization for suiseki clubs and individual members, it is a great honor for me to introduce this comprehensive work of art. Biologically speaking, stones are lifeless creatures. However, owing to man's primeval aspiration to shape, he has always understood that they were full of "inner life." Just as gems seem to live through the radiance of their light and fire, the particular beauty of these stones, shaped by nature, will seem completely different after you read this book. Creation itself is the force behind the mystic vitality of these objects, compressed by immeasurable forces which cut, carved, and shaped reliefs. Previously, people viewed stones as objects for mineral and fossil collections. Here we have a totally different picture. **Stones as works of art!**

We know that in old Shintoist Japan, people worshipped stones as divine beings. In Zen Buddhism, different stone compositions became important elements in the art of the garden. Stones retain their appearance over thousands of years. In them, we see something immutable and constant from the divine presence of nature. Just as a stone from one of the famous stone gardens attracts the attention of the observer through its own magic, an intense experience with suiseki conveys a feeling of the cosmic order to which man belongs. A suiseki is not simply a miniaturization of nature; nor is it only an accompaniment for bonsai. Suiseki are works of art in which cosmic forces are concentrated.

The author presents and describes the symbolism of these sometimes simple stones in a comprehensive and comprehensible manner. An appreciation of suiseki helps to maintain our capacity for relaxation. If we contemplate and experience these stones, in which the divine presence of nature has taken form, we feel an inner enrichment. This book should sustain efforts to make suiseki and Far Eastern art and philosophy understandable.

Like the bonsai lover, the suiseki collector remains attached to various cultural habits. This book delivers an exemplary overview and a competent explanation of concepts and notions which can sometimes only be imprecisely translated from Japanese into English. With its simple and concrete presentations and explanations, this book is an appropriate vehicle for introducing suiseki to interested people who have no previous knowledge of this art form. It contains attractive pictures showing what experienced suiseki collectors in the Far East have achieved, and it indicates what people in the West can expect with their conditions and perceptions.

The author succeeds in presenting and describing the art of suiseki in an attractive and uncomplicated way. In its concentrated form, suiseki is a space for meditation, an expression of unique proximity, and an intense experience with nature. It also expresses an awareness of the necessity for man and nature to coexist.

Stones are spiritual beings, images of nature, or images of subjects closely related to nature. When we see a stone as a miniature image, as a "copy of nature," we actively take part in this creation, and it suddenly appears that we are no longer the central point of creation.

Once more, I would like to congratulate Mr. Willi Benz and his "private secretary," Ms. Gudrun Benz, for this work. In addition to knowledge and judgment, the book contains definitions and criteria for measuring quality. These are important for the beginner, as well as for the longstanding enthusiast. I venture to conclude with the words of the old master and "bonsai ambassador," John Yoshio Naka:

"Man has to find the point of interest in a suiseki. After many hours or maybe days of imagining, the stone will reveal what it has to offer. The stone has stayed still all this time, but man's mind has been moved by this object, and it is this feeling or concept that brings great satisfaction from and appreciation for the culture of the Far East."

Norry Kirschten
President of the European Suiseki Association
President of the Bonsai Club of Luxembourg

Suiseki
A Short Description

Fundamentally, suiseki are stone objects shaped by nature. The influence of water, wind, sand, storms, and other natural forces turns some stones into miniature landscapes, shapes of extraordinary beauty with strong powers of suggestion, all contained in a few inches (see Fig. 1).

Suiseki is the Japanese term for these objects. Literally translated, *sui* means "water" and *seki* means "stone." But this does not express the true significance of suiseki as an art form. Instead, we should discover and interpret the "faces" of stones by observing them.

Today, we can describe in a relatively precise manner the physiological process that occurs between the eyes and the brain when we look at a picture. But we cannot reduce bonsai and suiseki to these external descriptions. We also cannot reduce these arts to a good realization technique. What we need is more of a mental process which often extends over long periods of time for a given object and the requisite cultural background. Then, many small details ripen and become, aesthetically speaking, comparable to a precious pearl necklace. Generally, such a process extends over many years. At the end of his life, the honest art lover realizes that he is only at the beginning. If we do not have the desire to sift what we see, this process will break down and cease. Therefore, we must think of suiseki as an endless intellectual experience.

FIG. 1 Japanese mountain range. A landscape stone with the preferred silky black tone. (Collection of G. Benz, 7 inches long.)

FIG. 2 Many Chinese gardens reproduce the legendary islands of Penglai. Here, we see them in the West Lake of Xihu in Hangzhou.

FIG. 3 A home display of beautiful and valuable objects, such as teapots, seals, small ceramic figures, and sui-seki.

FIG. 4 A tunnel stone on an elaborate wooden base (in Japanese, this is called a *daiza*). Hercules has placed the world on this stone while he rests. (Collection of M. Paiman, Jakarta, 13 inches high.)

Though stones do not change, new interpretations are always possible. The art of suiseki is a very rewarding hobby. Unlike bonsai, it is an inexpensive hobby which most people can enjoy. You can find stones which you will want to display as suiseki everywhere in nature. Most nature lovers find beautiful stones during their trips. With the advice from this book, simple stones will become very nice suiseki, as long as they fulfill certain conditions.

In the following chapters ("Historical Elements" and "Aesthetic Considerations"), we will include the Chinese and Japanese approaches to this art. Suiseki dates back more than two thousand years in China, where people placed small stones of exceptional natural beauty on bases. They were supposed to represent, for instance, the legendary Penglai Islands

(see Fig. 2), which were said to be approximately 435 miles north of Shanghai, off the coast of Shandong, the sacred mountains of Buddhism and Taoism. In the sixth century, these stones came to Japan by way of Korea. Since then, people have continued to develop the art of display. For centuries, people in other places in the world have also collected beautiful stones, but they have never displayed the stones so beautifully (see Fig. 3).

Presented on artistic tables or bases, suiseki embellish homes and gardens. They are a visual attraction, even a decorative central point. We call suiseki presented in the home "indoor suiseki" (see Fig. 4) and those for the garden, "outdoor suiseki" (see Figs. 5, 6). This particular art form is now practiced in many countries and can be compared with the concept of modern

FIG. 5 An outdoor sui-
seki in the garden, shaped
like an open oyster.
(Collection of P.
Adijuwono, Jakarta.)

paintings and sculptures (see Fig. 7). Beautiful bonsai or ikebana compositions, presented with a suiseki as a counterbalance, are special experiences of nature which transmit *joie de vivre* and harmony.

Suiseki are works of art which always bring much pleasure through sight, but we can also experience them through touch,

FIG. 6 For centuries, nature has worked on this outdoor suiseki to produce its well-proportioned shape. The stone weighs over 2,000 pounds. (Collection of M. Hartono, Bogor, 31½ inches high.)

which means that the visually impaired can enjoy them. Because they are immutable, suiseki produce a certain peacefulness which descends on the viewer after a long observation. In our hectic age, we can create a place of inner meditation and quiet with the help of suiseki.

The fascination and power of expression of suiseki should be perfectly natural. Any mechanical intervention by man must be rejected. Artificial changes are acceptable in only exceptional cases to create an even base. People consider suiseki to be masterpieces and, like other works of art, to be investments. Outstanding pieces can be worth thousands of dollars (see Fig. 8). The age of a suiseki helps to determine its value.

FIG. 7 Once again, nature was the sculptor. This work could be in a museum for contemporary art. (Collection of W. Benz, 8¼ inches high.)

FIG. 8 A valuable Japanese water pool stone with a representation of Buddha (on the right) and chrysanthemum flowers. These flowers are crystals deeply embedded in the stone. (Collection of Ms. Paiman, Jakarta, 15¾ inches long.)

FIG. 9 Miniature landscape (*penjing*) in the Yun Xiu Yuan garden ("The Garden of the Hidden Beauties") in Singapore. These stone landscapes represent a tradition that goes back 2,000 years in China.

FIG. 10 Alpine range in a *suiban* filled with silvery sand on a marmoreal tray. The stone was found in Liguria in northern Italy, close to a lake. This is a large karstic area in which people have found stones of various shapes. (Collection of W. Zimmer, Germany, 27½ inches long.)

The age refers to the time when the suiseki was first appreciated as a work of art, not to its geological age. In some Asian countries, presidents and prime ministers present beautiful suiseki as gifts during state visits. Often families pass down valuable pieces from one generation to the next. The power of expression, the harmony, the maturity, and the character of a suiseki express its true value in the universe.

Historical Elements

The shaping of miniature landscapes (see Fig. 9) or bonsai (see Fig. 11), and the display of suiseki (see Fig. 10) represent the original perception of the world in the Far East. However, they also contribute to art, because they only require the viewer to enjoy simple things and to develop a taste for the charm of apparently ordinary situations. In addition, they offer an opportunity to discover the beauty of nature and to

FIG. 11 A silver willow (*Pemphis acidula*) as a bonsai in the Yun Xiu Yuan garden in Singapore.

study more profound subjects. In this way, we can transcend the limits of our conventional thinking. Through their diversity of shapes, colors, and impressions, suiseki are a source of endless inspiration.

The art of suiseki is an intentional exercise in beauty and harmony which requires a creative process. When added to the rhythm of everyday life, leisure time with suiseki offers both a visual consciousness and a regenerative pause.

From ancient times until today, these values have filled the spirit and created harmony; their charm continues to fascinate the observer.

The Japanese concept of *furyu* roughly translates to "elegant entertainment." In Chinese, this concept, called *feng-liu*, or "following the wind," defines the way of life of ancient Chinese scholars. In periods of unruliness, they turned away from rigid Confucian morals and found comfort in Buddhism or Taoism. Strictly speaking, *feng-liu* means to adapt oneself to the stream of life as if to a blast of wind. This enables one to forget all the contradictions assaulting the mind and to identify oneself with nature. In the third century A.D., Yuan Chi, one of the seven wise men of the "Wood of Bamboo," expressed his

FIG. 12 Yuan Chi, one of the seven wise men of the "Wood of Bamboo," in his rustic solitude. Here, he enjoyed the natural pleasure of looking at beautiful stones.

16

dislike for rigid conventions. He retired into the mountains and enjoyed the beauties of nature, especially beautiful stones (see Fig. 12).

For many people in our bustling world, contact with nature has become almost a necessity of life. Suiseki art can help by offering us the opportunity to spiritually take off our "city clothes" and become one with nature.

But this entertainment and serenity do not indicate an absence of activity. On the contrary, suiseki art brings about a spiritual contact with the highest values, enabling us to accept the physical work required by life and helping us to cleanse our minds.

The Chinese, and later the Japanese, who were influenced by Chinese culture, interpreted the cyclic changes in states of the mind caused by nature as changes in the relations between Yin and Yang (see Fig. 13).

Those who believe in this Chinese system of Yin and Yang, called *in-yo* by the Japanese, explain the natural forces by using the action of two opposing yet complementary principles. A suiseki landscape in a *suiban* (ceramic tray) filled with water symbolizes the two natural forces of the universe. The stone represents Yang characteristics, and water symbolizes Yin.

Yin, the feminine principle, is related to the concepts of wet, cold, smooth, mysterious, passive, dark, moon, earth, and north. Originally, it meant the shadowy side of the mountain.

Yang, the male principle, is related to the concepts of light, sun, blue sky, emperor, dragon, dryness, hard, solid, clear, shiny, south, and all the uneven numbers.

As key elements of the Chinese cosmology, the concepts of Yin and Yang are so strongly related to one another that one cannot exist without the other. Humans have always tried to maintain Yin and Yang in harmony.

A conscious perception of nature

FIG. 13 Eight diagrams with the Yin Yang symbol at the center. The eight diagrams are the basic forms for all the diagrams in the "Book of Transforma-tions I-Ging." Both natural forces, the female Yin and the male Yang, come from the Original Being. Together, they produced the Five Elements, which are the origin of the Ten Thousand Things. The concept of Yin and Yang comes to us from Asia.

encourages creation. Thus, poetry, painting, bonsai, and suiseki became unique elements of the culture of the Far East.

Under the influence of Zen in the fourteenth and fifteenth centuries, *feng-liu* acquired a special significance. It influenced the Japanese aesthetics so deeply that we still admire its results today, for example, in their marvelous gardens (see Fig. 14), unique stone placements, tea ceremonies, and suiseki displays.

Borrowed from the Chinese, this "fruitful atmosphere" has supported the development of the typical Japanese attitude towards beauty and harmony. Over the course of time, this attitude has penetrated into every class of society and into almost every area of everyday life. The Japanese are looking for the significance of human life not only in the future but also in the full experience of the present. This fact is worth a moment of reflection.

FIG. 14   View of the wonderful garden of Ryogen In in Kyoto.

Feng-liu (*furyu* in Japanese) became an aesthetic notion and a symbol for refined elegance and highest praise. This was the case, for example, when someone described a suiseki as *furyu*. The word also refers to a specific way of life in which one avoids ostentation as an obstacle to finding peace for the soul. One cultivates an "educated poverty" to satisfy immediate aesthetic needs.

The internal significance of a process or composition is indeed expressed in the simplest manner. But this simplicity does not mean mental poverty or lack of fantasy. On the contrary, it has a rich content. For this reason, Japanese artists, such as traditional painters, haiku poets, bonsai makers, and suiseki artists, became masters of allusion and incomplete expression.

In Japan, writing, reading, and listening to lyric poems have been valued for centuries as national traditions. This includes tanka and haiku. Both are short poem forms.

Tanka is a poem form which has five stanzas and thirty-one syllables.

Haiku is a poem form which has three stanzas and seventeen syllables.

The lyric poem has only one phrase and must find its full artistic expression in this short form. Haiku came from tanka; the last two stanzas were dropped, leaving only three stanzas. In the fifteenth century, poets used this form to emphasize the artistic effect of the unexpressed, incomplete, and hinted. Moreover, each haiku refers to one of the five following periods of the year: new year, spring, summer, autumn, or winter.

> *Evening was clear*
> *Before the unclouded sky*
> *Mountains, autumn blue.*
> *(Issa)*

The constant use of fine and subtle improvisations with corresponding objects in different arts led to an endless variety of

18

FIG. 15 Landscape painting from south China using a watercolor technique that is 150 years old.

compositions, none of which descended to the ordinary. By combining different shapes, materials, and colors, Japanese artists demonstrated their creative powers. An essential element in all work was the sparsely furnished room.

FIG. 13 The use of asymmetry avoids a rigid display of art.

FIG. 17 A *tokonoma*, or "art alcove," in a Japanese house, where works of art with special value are displayed. Generally, a tokonoma only includes two or three objects in a carefully balanced relationship. The display has three levels: above (in the background) is a scroll with a landscape painting that is an ink drawing, *sumi-e* in Japanese; at the intermediary level is a landscape suiseki; and next to the suiseki is a complementary plant.

This sparseness forces the observer to dig further, beyond the surface of things. Of course, the digging requires the viewer's active cooperation in the artistic process. The typical asymmetry plays an important role in the process (see Fig. 16). The Japanese believe that symmetry destroys inspiration because it contradicts nature and is normally the result of human work. The perfect example of asymmetry is its use in the *sukiya*, the room in which the tea ceremony is performed. It is a place of emptiness and asymmetry and also a place of imagination. The room is devoid of ostentation, and the only articles in the room are there solely to satisfy an aesthetic need.

In addition to bonsai, ikebana, and scrolls, suiseki, with their simple elegance, also have much to contribute to the success of a tea ceremony.

The tea room is a place of asymmetry because it is devoted to the veneration of the imperfect, and imperfection provides room for the imagination.

Since the sixteenth century, the ideals of the tea ceremony have influenced Japanese architects. In fact, most foreigners find the usual Japanese interior architecture bare or insufficient because of its apparent simplicity and the modesty of its decoration.

FIG. 18 Miniature landscape—*saikei*. In earlier times, these landscapes were very popular in Japan. Then they were forgotten. However, they were rediscovered in the middle of the twentieth century. (Collection of S. Kato.)

The first independent tea room was created by Sen no Sôekti, the greatest of all tea masters. He is usually called by his later name, Rikyû. In the sixteenth century, with the support of Taikô Hideyoshi, Rikyû developed the external form of the tea ceremony and brought it to its highest perfection. Shô-ô, a famous tea master of the fifteenth century, had already defined the size and proportions of the tea room.

At the beginning, the tea room was part of the usual sitting room, separated by a screen during the tea celebration.

The separated room was called *kakoi*, or "cell," a name still used for tea rooms built in the house rather than as a separate building.

In the *sukiya*, we find the tearoom itself, designed for no more than five people, a number which permitted the use of the expression "more than the Graces and less than the Muses."

There is an entry room (*mizuya*) where tea tools are washed and prepared for use, a waiting room (*machiai*) where guests wait until they are called into the tea room, and a garden path (*roji*), which links the *machiai* and the tea room. The tea room appears to be quite simple.

It is smaller than the smallest Japanese house, and its building materials are cho-sen to suggest an impression of "educated poverty."

However, we must realize that this impression is the result of artistic planning. All details are chosen with as much care as would go into building the finest palace. A good tea room is more expensive than an ordinary house because the choice of materials and the building itself require extraordinary care and precision.

In a tea room, we find the *tokonoma*, an art alcove (see Fig. 17). This is the place of honor in a Japanese room, and, at the same time, it is the archetype of a Zen chapel altar. The size of a tea room is defined in the Buddhist sutra, *Vikramaditya*.

It is equal in size to four and a half *tatami* matting, or 10 square feet. Often, a scroll hangs in the *tokonoma*. In front of the scroll, a suiseki and a complementary plant are displayed. In addition, we often find bonsai or ikebana in the *tokonoma*.

Placing the objects in the room so that they produce a harmonious balance which the visitor can perceive is considered an art form of its own.

In order to create the proper impression, certain rules must be followed (see "Display and Exhibition of Suiseki and Bonsai"). Here too, asymmetry plays an essential part.

21

FIG. 19 This miniature mountain range shows the ravaged face of time and, with its numerous folds, can be classified as a near-view mountain stone. (Collection of M. Paiman, Jakarta, 20 inches long.)

The ancient Japanese worshipped certain stones and rock formations as the residences of various spirits, gods, and natural forces. Under the influence of Buddhism, people valued these stones for their hardness, solidity, and other inner features. For Buddhists, they symbolized the sacred mountain, Shumi, around which the world turns. For Taoists, these stones represented the mythological paradise, the sacred mountain Horai. The Chinese appreciation of penjing and the Japanese of *saikei* (see Fig. 18) have also been influenced by the original religions of China and Japan, Taoism and Shintoism. But the Koreans also worshipped stones that nature had stamped in a special way. They often circle these stones with a rope fringed with paper strips. One sees such stones near Suwon, south of Seoul.

The Japanese worship the "Wedded Rocks" (Myoto-iwa) on the Futamigaura coast near Ise. They view them as jewels of Shintoism. These two rocks symbolize Izanagi and Izanami, the mythological founders of Japan. Every year, the Japanese renew the robe of plaited straw which symbolizes the holy marriage.

Later, influenced by the Chinese, the Koreans and Japanese considered these stones as comforting objects. Even today, people offer sacrifices to such stones.

Unfortunately, old Japanese literature rarely mentions the art of suiseki. However, one sometimes finds mention of outstanding stones. There is a report that Empress Suiko (593–628 A.D.) received a miniature landscape stone as a gift from the Chinese emperor's court. This miniature landscape stone and other stones imported from China had fantastic shapes. They had deep marks and furrows, and they bore the ravaged face of time (see Fig. 19). During the centuries that followed, odd-looking stones became collectors' items and important import goods.

Another source, the *Ise Monogatari* (800–900 A.D.), provides the first mention of suiseki in Japan, called *sazare ishi*. This Stone was found near Wakayama. It was given as a gift to the emperor Seiwa (850–881 A.D.) and has been passed down to each succeeding emperor. Today, it is a treasured piece in the Fukuoji temple of Asabe (Hiroshima).

Although the art of suiseki originated in China, it is now practiced in all the countries of the Far East. There are suiseki clubs in Indonesia, Japan, Korea, Taiwan, Hong Kong, Malaysia, and Singapore. Club members and many state museums possess significant collections of suiseki (see Fig. 20). In addition to those in the Far East, enthusiasts have established suiseki clubs in the United States, Canada, South Africa, New

FIG. 20 An especially beautiful black stone with brown markings in a *doban* (bronze tray) filled with white sand. This type of tray is generally reserved for "noble stones." We can see the small tunnel on the right side. (Collection of M. Paiman, Jakarta.)

Zealand, Australia, and Europe. The first public exhibition of suiseki in Europe took place in 1992 in Monaco. Today, many European cities have suiseki clubs. All such clubs exchange information and knowledge, and most organize exhibitions periodically to share their appreciation of this art with the public.

Unfortunately, there is no agreed upon title for this art form. The word or words vary from country to country. Chance has often played a part in determining the designation in a given place. For example,

people in Europe learned about this art form from the Japanese, and they use the Japanese term, "suiseki." In China, where suiseki originated, people refer to it as *shangsek,* "enjoyable stone." In Taiwan, it is called *ya-sek,* "beautiful artistic stone." Koreans use *useok,* "eternal stone." In the United States, we find at least three designations, including "viewing stone," "panorama stone," and "loving stone." Indonesia, Hong Kong, and the Philippines use the term "suiseki."

Aesthetic Considerations

FIG. 21   Japanese tea garden in the park of the Nijo castle in Kyoto. From the terrace of the tea house on the right, one gazes on this scene.

Under the influence of Zen, Japanese gardens, which had been previously designed to be cheerful and amusing, became monochromatic landscapes, similar to the paintings of the Sung period (see Fig. 21). This change reflected the respect of nature expressed by Taoism and Buddhism. Scholars tried to convey this sense of nature, and they expressed themselves by creating gardens or collecting beautiful stones. Above all, they respected open nature. If they intended to "domesticate" nature for home display (in the form of a beautiful stone), this feeling of naturalness had to be preserved as much as possible. Surprisingly, it was the monochrome ink drawings of the Sung period which had the biggest

influence on this philosophy (see Fig. 22). From then on, and especially at the beginning and in the middle of the fourteenth century, Japanese Zen monks felt that stone arrangements in flat trays (*suiban*) filled with water or sand, as well as suiseki, should also be monochromes. This monochrome, ranging from light gray to deep black, is clearly evidence of the monochromatic shades of ink drawing (*sumi-e*).

Chinese painters of the Tang and Sung dynasties were the first to discover that they could capture all the colors of nature while using only black tint. The illusion is so perfect that sometimes the observer has to force himself to remember that he is not looking at a polychromatic scene.

山高水長
戊辰歲春作
張峰題於
乾春

FIG. 22 A Chinese silk painting in
the style of the Sung ink painting. We
can clearly identify the three-level perspective. The artist, Zhang Feng, is a
famous Chinese painter who has mas-
tered traditional Chinese landscape
painting. His atelier is in the
monastery of Shaolin, where karate
was developed.

FIG. 23 A typical monochrome suiseki in a precious bronze tray. (Collection of M. Paiman.)

FIG. 24 The large sand surface around the stone gives the impression of a vast tract. The stone is classified as a slope stone. (Collection of R. Nakayama.)

The Japanese art critic Seiroku Noma wrote in 1957: "At first sight, these few ink markings on white paper seem annoying and uninteresting, but the more we look at them, the more they arrange themselves into an image of nature. At first, this small piece of nature is rather indistinct, as though viewed through a foggy sheet, but then the mind perceives a superb whole. Ink drawing reduces all the colors of nature to shades of black, but it paradoxically succeeds in suggesting precisely the true color shades..." The mind of a suiseki lover is moved in the same way when he observes a monochromatic suiseki.

FIG. 25 The same stone is represented in these three pictures. In the first picture, the size of the tray is properly proportioned to the size of the stone. In the second picture, the tray is too small; and in the third one, it is too large.

FIG. 26 A view of the famous dry garden, Ryôanji. This *kare sansui*, or dry landscape, dates from the year 1490. It contains fifteen stones, but the viewer cannot see all the stones from any one place. Here is a world of unique charm.

Japanese artists emphasize the impression of size and depth of a garden by leaving large empty places. This emptiness seems to enlarge the field of view (see Fig. 26). In the same way, we place suiseki in very flat trays to create the impression of a large space (see Fig. 24). To produce this effect, the tray must be at least twice as long as the stone (see Fig. 25). We embed the suiseki in the gravel of the tray so that it appears as if it were an iceberg coming into view from an endless depth.

In some cases, one can also embed a suiseki in very fine moss, as if nature had thrown it there. In this case, the moss bed is not uniform; some irregularities remain. The observer associates this with untouched nature. A "suiseki realization" should appear unplanned in order to weaken the critical capacity of the viewer's intelligence and to deceive the viewer so that he experiences a feeling of unlimited space and depth. This symbolic representation of the cosmos in such a small space produces a sensation of eternity. Like the dry landscapes (*kare sansui*) created with gravel and stones in the last decade of the fifteenth century, suiseki creations composed in a similar way can also be the last step in reproducing Sung pictures in space, a concentration of the universe in the smallest space.

With this aim in mind, only stones which bear the ravaged face of time are appropriate. Long, furrowed stones are valued because of their resemblance to high, steep mountain ranges.

FIG. 27 A brown and beige suiseki in a precious ancient Chinese *suiban*. (Collection of R. Nakayama.)

For suiseki realizations in trays (*suiban*), simplicity, understatement, strength, and restraint are important. The famous dry garden, Ryôanji, in Kyoto (see Fig. 26), created in 1490, is an example of such a display. It represents a symbolic mountain panorama. In addition, in the language of painting, it is an abstract piece of art on a gravel "canvas" which transcends the symbolic representation of a landscape and offers a view of the whole universe at the highest level of abstraction. Neither pictures nor words can adequately describe this garden. However, it breathes a spirit, which no one can ignore. People who visit this garden and experience its quiet will be moved, even if they have no knowledge of Zen painting or Zen realization.

The style was borrowed from Chinese painting by the Japanese of the Ashikaga period (1333–1573). It consists of creating all nuances of light and shade with black tint in order to attain more expressive and deeper effects. Therefore, many Japanese suiseki lovers prefer a palette of gray to black for their suiseki.

However, this does not mean that suiseki lovers limit themselves to gray or black stones. On the contrary, their collections contain the whole rainbow. For instance, some very valuable suiseki have color tones varying from light brown or beige to dark brown (see Fig. 27). These usually possess other features of a suiseki, such as strength, shape, texture, and balance.

The continuous changes in nature and the diversity of shapes, colors, and expressions are sources of permanent inspiration. Suiseki, bonsai, ikebana, and landscape creations in trays are unique expressions of Asian world perception. As art forms, they allow us to enjoy apparently ordinary things. This, in turn, allows us to transcend spatial thinking, which is limited by convention. The domains of landscape penjing, bonsai, suiseki, and ikebana are conscious exercises of beauty.

Since the third century, Chinese scholars have cultivated a way of life called *feng-liu*, "following the wind." This notion, called *furyu* in Japan, could be translated simply as "elegant entertainment."

Feng-liu, or *furyu*, also means adapting oneself to the stream of life.

FIG. 28 The famous ninety-two-year-old Chinese animal painter Beisi Qi finishing a calligraphy in his "paradise." The calligraphy on the wall is the word "paradise."

A life spent in close contact with nature brought experiences which were opportunities for creative activities. People collected suiseki, created landscapes in containers, cultivated miniature trees, wrote poems and essays, painted pictures, or made calligraphy (see Fig. 28). The unique heritage of fourteenth-century Chinese culture is fascinating to observe. In the fourteenth century, *feng-liu* came to Japan, where the concept, now called *furyu* / or "elegant entertainment," fell under the influence of Zen teaching.

In Japan, many people abandoned their active lives after having attained a level of spiritual maturity, and devoted themselves only to their hobbies, that is to say to "following the wind."

Furyu is also an aesthetic concept roughly equivalent to the concept of cultivated elegance, similar to the expressions *shibui* and *shibusa*. When we say that a suiseki possesses *furyu* or *shibui*, we mean that it expresses simplicity and noble elegance. A composition consisting of a complementary plant, a suiseki, and a picture which simply indicates the remote beauty of nature, might suggest the slight breeze of a summer evening. The composition brings the very essence of this natural experience into the home.

Aesthetic Concepts

Feng-Liu (Chinese)—

"Following the wind," or "elegant entertainment," was the way of life of the Chinese scholars in the Middle Ages.

Furyu-(Japanese)—

"Elegant entertainment" or "noble elegance" were similar to the terms of *shibui* and *shibusa*.

Sabi-(Japanese)—

This concept cannot be described precisely. It includes the notions of ancient, respectable, antique, mature, melancholic, lonely, subdued, and seasoned.

However, *sabi* also designates an understanding of the transitory nature of things, which are beautiful precisely because they are fleeting, for example, the beauty of a suiseki or of a bonsai which becomes older with time.

Shibui (Japanese)—

This concept is difficult to define. It includes the concepts of quiet, elegance, understated, reserved, reflective, polished, and refined.

Wabi (Japanese)—

This is another concept which is difficult to translate. It includes the notions of simple, lonely, melancholic, quiet, desolate, impoverished, and unpretentious. It is the subjective impression evoked by a picture of a lonely fisherman's shack buffeted by a storm on a gray winter day. An undefined mournful impression is penetrated by the enjoyment of the magic contained in most simple things.

Wabi is a feeling of the simplicity and naturalness of things. Together, sabi and wabi convey an impression of quiet and serenity.

Yoin (Japanese)—

Literally, *yoin* means "echoing." When a gong is struck in a temple, it continues to sound for long after the actual strike. When we are fascinated by a suiseki or a bonsai and cannot forget the experience, we call this impression *yoin*, a strong, impressive power.

Yugen (Japanese)—

Here is another concept that we cannot define precisely. It includes darkness, obscurity, mystery, uncertainty, profoundness, and subtlety. Examples include subjective pictures such as the moon shining behind a veil of clouds or a mountain veiled by the morning mist.

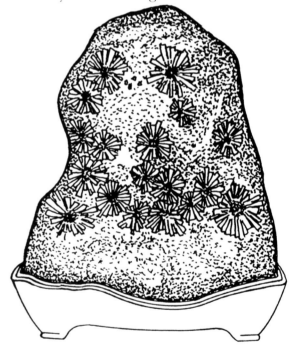

Stylistic Classification of Suiseki

After acquiring about ten objects, all art collectors seem to stop and consider the criteria for building their collection. This was often a problem for suiseki collectors because there was no worldwide standard classification. During the many centuries when the art of suiseki was evolving, it was influenced by cultural and spiritual trends which came from other arts.

However, we can identify certain typical basic properties, such as the mineralogical structure, the shape, and the color which a stone must possess to be considered as a suiseki. Moreover, we can define the stylistic elements which make suiseki classification possible. In Japan, sizes describe the width, the depth, and the height (see Fig. 29). In Korea, the sequence is width, height, and then depth.

The classification follows a simple pattern. In fact, this is the result of a compromise, and so it is a combination of the Chinese, Japanese, and Korean systems of classification.

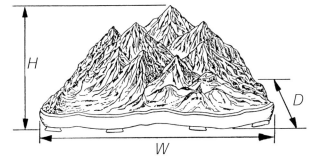

FIG. 29 Drawing showing the dimensions as they are generally given for suiseki. However, the sequence is not uniform from country to country. W = width/length, H = height, D = depth.

I. Shape

    A. Landscape stones (mountains, mountain ranges, etc.)

    B. Object stones (man, animal, house, etc.)

II. Surface patterns

    A. Human
    B. Animal
    C. Plant
    D. Landscape
    E. Celestial
    F. Weather
    G. Abstract

III. Place of origin

IV. Color

Detailed Classification

In addition to listing their English terms, we've listed Japanese names for most categories. These end with the term *ishi* or *seki*, both of which mean "stone" or "stones." The Japanese name for a stone can also contain the word *gata*, which is a generic designation for "form" or "in the form of."

The classification sequence for landscape stones has been chosen so that the first thing the observer who enters the landscape sees is the mountains in the distance. Then, he recognizes rivers, waterfalls, etc. Moreover, we present the classification for landscape stones first, and only then the one for object stones because, historically, man perceived the surrounding nature first and then specific objects.

Shape

Landscape Stones

sansui kei-seki; sansui keijo-seki (see Fig. 30)

FIG. 30 This suiseki reminds me of a landscape in Nepal. It was once the "Hanging Gardens" with a farmhouse (left, bottom third) which especially impressed me. (Collection of W. Benz, 4¾ inches long.)

Mountain or mountain range stones

yamagata-ishi

Mountains seen from a great distance

toyama-ishi; enzan-seki (see Fig. 31)

During a walk in the highlands, if we observe mountains in the distance, the first thing we see are their outlines. Then, we begin to see linear structures, but these only indicate the main shapes. We cannot recognize the finer structures because the mountains are too far away. Suiseki belonging to this group are single mountains or mountain ranges with several peaks.

FIG. 31 This is a distant mountain stone. We can only recognize the outline of the mountain. This special stone quality is called *makko-ishi* in Japan and is especially prized. (Collection of W. Benz, 7⅞ inches long.)

FIG. 32 In this drawing of a distant mountain stone, the peaks have different heights and are marked by folds and ridges.

Those stones with white flecks or veins are especially prized and suggest patterned "snow fields," raging rivers, or clouds. Also highly valued are stones that represent single mountains with a prominent peak that lies at point forty percent along the total length.

The most prized mountain stones have an odd number of asymmetrical triangular peaks in various heights and shapes. Ideally, the front and back of the stone should have different slopes (see Fig. 31). Mountain ranges with an even number of peaks are not desirable because they do not respect the rule of asymmetry. The peaks should not be situated on a single straight line, and they should be naturally placed around the main peak tiers (see Fig. 32). The mountains should be steeper at their peaks than at their bases. Moreover, the angles of the front and back sides should be different. Having a steeper front side than back side is preferable. To create a better sense of depth, the back side of the stone should have peaks that are more round than the ones in the front. The pointed peaks and deep folds should be placed so that they are in the front. These mountains and mountain ranges represent intimate pictures. This is the reason why even people who have never heard of suiseki appreciate them.

FIG. 33 This fantastic alpine mountain range is only 15 inches long. Found in northern Italy, it is a typical near-view mountain stone with ideal proportions and ridges. (Collection of W. Benz.)

Near-view mountain stones

kinzan-seki (see Fig. 33)

As we walk towards a mountain, the outlines and folds become progressively sharper. A suiseki classified in this group must possess all the characteristics of a near-view mountain or mountain range. It must also have rough, cracked outlines, marked peaks, and steep, abrupt walls (see Fig. 34).

Island mountain stones

Island mountains (see Fig. 35) are solitary mountains which stand on large plains; for suiseki, this means on a flat stone plate. We distinguish between sugarloaf island mountains (see Fig. 36) and shield island mountains. These latter have a flat rise similar to the battle shield of a knight (see Fig. 35). Stones like the one shown in Fig. 36 are rather rare.

FIG. 34 The drawing shows a near-view mountain with nine marked peaks.

FIG. 35 The drawing shows a shield island mountain on the left and a sugarloaf island mountain on the right.

FIG. 36   This sugarloaf island mountain lies on a stone plate, a vast plain. (Collection of Luciana Garbini, Italy, 7 inches long.)

FIG. 37   Bare basalt mountains emerging from the snow and glacier fields of the North Cape. We can easily see a glacier on the front. (Collection of Bonsai Centrum, Heidelberg, 5 inches long.)

Mountain stones with ice and snow or glaciers (see Fig. 37)

Stones with white peaks, spots, or veins are especially prized because these markings suggest snow fields, glaciers, clouds, or streams. Stones with white peaks (Fig. 38) are also valued, as are stones with flat calcite or quartz veins that are wider at the foot. These suggest descending glaciers or large snow fields.

Fig. 38 Mountain range with snow-covered peaks.

FIG. 40 Mountain with two lakes. We've added a drop of milk so that the lakes are more prominent. (Collection of W. Benz, 9 inches long.)

Mountain stones with one or more lakes (Fig. 39)

To suggest mountain lakes, such stones must have one or more distinct hollows that you can fill with water. With black stones, we sometimes add a drop of milk

This is very similar to what we find in nature. The highest peak for this type of stone should be situated at about forty percent of the total length. Especially beauti-

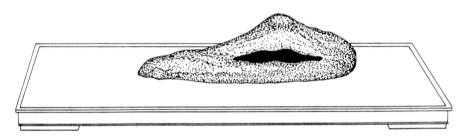

FIG. 39 Distant mountain stone with a lake.

to make the lakes more prominent. This increases the contrast between stone and water, but it is less natural. However, without the addition of milk to the water, you'd have a difficult time seeing the small lake on the left (see Fig. 40). The most valued stones have background mountains which are much higher than the water level of the lake.

ful stones have lake shapes that are similar to the shape of the stone. This means that elongated stones should also have elongated lakes. We usually observe suiseki with one or several mountain lakes from a normal perspective. This means an angle of about 5–20 degrees (see Fig. 213), which allows us to see the contours of the water surface.

FIG. 41 Suiseki with a diagonal mountain stream running through the stone. The stream becomes wider at the bottom. The stone has ideal proportions. However, it is placed too far to the right on the suiban. If the stone were placed with its visual central point more to the left so that it is above the golden section of the tray, this would be a perfect display.

Mountain stream stones

keiryu-seki (see Fig. 41)

We can find mountains with streams and rivers descending on their slopes everywhere in the world. A stone's white veins should appear to be foaming, plunging water (see Fig. 42). In the distance, we see light-colored water veins which stand out against the rather dark background. Mountain stream stones must reflect this natural flow with a similar shape.

Light quartz or calcite veins crossing the stone suggest streams and rivers. When these mineral veins are depressions in the stone (representing gorges, gullies, valleys), they appear more natural. Stones crossed diagonally by winding "rivers" or "streams" (see Fig. 41) are beautiful. The river should be narrower at the top and become progressively wider towards the bottom.

FIG. 42 A white, foaming mountain stream running through a rocky depression.

37

Waterfall Stones

FIG. 43 In this waterfall, the water winds down along the mountain slope and then plunges into the deep water below. This is an ideal model for a waterfall suiseki.

FIG. 45 A sheet waterfall. (Japanese garden in Freiburg, Germany.)

FIG. 46 Dry-waterfall suiseki in a suiban. (Collection of W. Benz, 6⅜ inches long.)

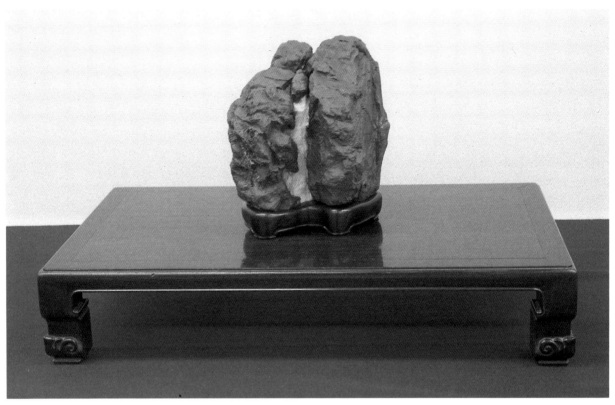

FIG. 44 A thread-waterfall suiseki. (Photograph taken during the suiseki exhibition in Tokyo in October 1993.)

FIG. 47 A dry-waterfall suiseki. The stone was found by my friend Zeng Zi Ping in the Pearl River in south China. (Collection of W. Benz, 10¼ inches long.)

Waterfall stones

taki-ishi

In nature, we see a number of different types of waterfall:

▮▮▮ The water runs down in threads (see Fig. 44).

▮▮▮ The water runs down in a sheet (see Fig. 45).

▮▮▮ The water runs down in two or more cascading steps (see Fig. 45).

▮▮▮ The water has dried up and is only indicated by the dry folds it has created (see Figs. 46, 47).

According to these observations, we classify waterfall stones as:

▮▮▮ **Thread-waterfall stones**—*itodaki-ishi* (see Fig. 44)

▮▮▮ **Sheet-waterfall stones**—*nunodaki-ishi* (see Fig. 45)

▮▮▮ **Waterfall stones with several cascading steps**

▮▮▮ **Dry-waterfall stones**—*karedaki-ishi* (see Figs. 46, 47)

The dry waterfall stones only show folds created by water. Stones with a high contrast between rock and "waterfall" (usually a quartz vein) are especially beautiful. In order to look natural, the quartz vein or mark symbolizing water must only be visible on the front side of the stone, and the water at the top of the waterfall should seem to wind its way down the stone.

Be cautious about buying such stones. People have offered to sell me stones on which they had artificially created waterfall with white paint or epoxy resin. Such an imitation is worthless.

Plateau stones

dan-seki or *dan-ishi* (see Fig. 48)

We can describe these stones as two or more plateaus together. Such suiseki have one or several flat levels with different heights. An uneven number of clearly distinct plateaus of different heights is ideal (see Fig. 49).

FIG. 48 Typical plateau stone in a *suiban*.

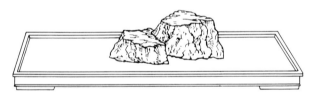

FIG. 49 Plateau stone with two plateaus and a mountain stream. (Photographed during the Second Asian Pacific Suiseki Exhibition in Hong Kong in 1993.)

Slope stones

doha-seki (see Fig. 50)

These suiseki have gently contoured slopes, as if a glacier had scraped them (see Fig. 51). They also have rounded shapes. Stones displayed in a *suiban* filled with sand are especially impressive.

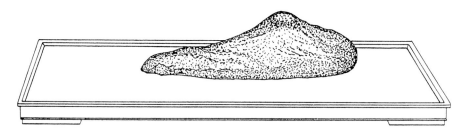

FIG. 50 This stone has the typical shape of a slope stone.

FIG. 51 A slope stone typical of the ones found in northwestern Italy. You can display these stones with a *daiza* or in a *suiban* filled with sand.

Shore stones

isogata-ishi (see Fig. 52)

The main characteristic is the presence of "feet" washed out by the power of the waves (see Fig. 53). During my trips, I have learned to recognize two typical shapes:

▌▌▌ Reef stones

araiso-seki (see Fig. 54)

Reef stones can take all possible shapes. They always have distinct erosion marks, and sometimes, odd-shaped surfaces.

▌▌▌ Sandbar stones

hirasu-ishi (see Fig. 55)

These stones must be very flat and slightly modeled. Sandbar stones are displayed in a *suiban* with water so that they just peer out of the water. Reef stones, on the other hand, are displayed in a *suiban* filled with sand.

FIG. 52 Shore stone in a *suiban*. Erosion marks caused by water and wind are generally easy to recognize.

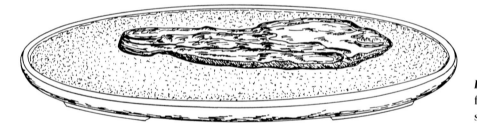

FIG. 53 Shore stone suiseki in a *suiban*. The surface is strongly eroded. Along the lower part, you can see the erosion marks made by water. (Stone is 11 inches long.)

FIG. 54 The action of the sea shaped this reef stone, creating the erosion marks.

FIG. 55 The sea creates flat sandbar stones. Here, sand symbolizes the sea.

Coastal rock stones

iwagata-ishi (see Fig. 56)

The surface of these stones is marked by wind and waves (see Fig. 57). High steep rocks (see Fig. 56) and massive, powerful stones (see Fig. 58) are especially impressive. Stones with quartz in their lower parts suggest the foam of the sea. These quartz veins should also have odd shapes.

During ebb tide, we often see coastal rocks surrounded by sand. We need to remember this when displaying a coastal rock stone in a *suiban*.

Island stones

shimagata-ishi

Island stones have a typical island shape protruding from the sea (see Fig. 59). Natural islands often have distinctive shapes carved by waves. Suiseki should also have this characteristic. You can create an especially beautiful display if you use a bluish green glaze on the bottom of the *suiban*, cover this only partially with sand, and fill it with soft water.

The suiseki will then symbolize an island with a beach and the surrounding sea.

FIG. 56 This high coastal rock shows strong erosion marks caused by the elements. (Collection of W. Benz, 4 inches high. Gift of Ms. Melba Tucker of California to promote the German Suiseki Society.)

FIG. 57 The erosion marks on coastal rocks depend on the elements, but they also depend on the type of stone. (Collection of W. Benz, 4¾ inches high.)

FIG. 58 We can easily see the erosion marks caused by the action of the sea in this powerful coastal rock stone. (Stone is 11 inches long.)

FIG. 59 Island stone in a *suiban* filled with sand. The sand symbolizes water. Koreans add water to the sand up to the rim. (Stone is 7⅞ inches long. Photograph taken during the Suiseki Exhibition in Tokyo in 1993.)

Cave stones

dokutsu-ishi (see Fig. 60)
Erosion from the waves of the sea has created caves or caverns (see Fig. 61). Ideal cave stones have dark caves, the ends of which the observer cannot see, suggesting great depth.

FIG. 60 Tana Lot on the island of Bali is a natural model for cave stones.

FIG. 61 This stone from Java shows distinct caverns and holes. (Collection of W. Benz, 9⅞ inches long.)

Shelter stones; overhanging cliff

yadori-ishi/amayadori-ishi

A rock overhang (see Fig. 62) is a natural protection against rain. Stones of this category must also have a natural base under the overhang where a man looking for refuge might seek shelter.

If this base is missing, we speak of an overhanging cliff (see Fig. 63). If the *daiza* had a longer base, the requirement of a shelter would have been fulfilled.

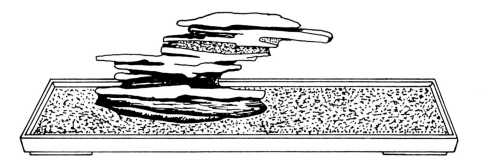

FIG. 62 Typical shape of an overhanging cliff. A man could use this as a temporary shelter from the rain.

FIG. 63 We usually replace the missing base on the left side of this overhanging cliff with a *daiza* of the same shape. We could also place a small stone plate in the spot where a man looking for refuge would stand.

FIG. 64 This spit of land is a natural model for a tunnel stone. We can clearly see that the water created the tunnel.

45

Tunnel stones

domon-ishi

We often find natural models for these stones in the national parks in the American Southwest (see Fig. 65), in the form of coastal rocks on the island of Bali (see Fig. 64), and in the Cevennes in France (Ardèche, Montpellier). A stone in this category must have at least one tunnel (see Figs. 66a, 66b).

We could also display the stone shown in Fig. 66a in a *suiban* filled with water (see Fig. 66b). In many places throughout the world, rock walls with two or more tunnels have been forming for thousands of years. This is also the case for miniature stones.

FIG. 65 The natural tunnel of the Rainbow Bridge in the Lake Powell region of the United States is the highest stone tunnel in the world. (The tunnel is 300 feet high.)

FIG. 65a A tunnel stone with a distinct tunnel. Although the stone is on a wooden base, it could also be displayed in a *suiban* filled with water. (Stone is 6¾ inches long.)

46

FIG. 66b This is the same stone shown in Fig. 66a. Now it is in a *suiban*. Normally, the *suiban* would contain water.

FIG. 67 This tunnel stone has two holes. It was found on the island of Java. Natural models are often found in the American Southwest. (Collection of G. Benz, 6 inches long.)

Water pool stones

mizutamari-ishi

Such stones are generally compared to the beautiful water pools found in Japanese gardens (*tsukubai*). To enhance this associa-tion, we can put a bamboo ladle on the stone (see Fig. 68). Unlike stones with lakes, these stones should have a large water area.

FIG. 68 This serpentine water pool stone in a suiban is 6 inches long. (Collection of H. Rundio, Germany.)

FIG. 69 This water pool stone was found in Java. The crayfish on the left side indicates water, even though the stone is not totally filled with water.

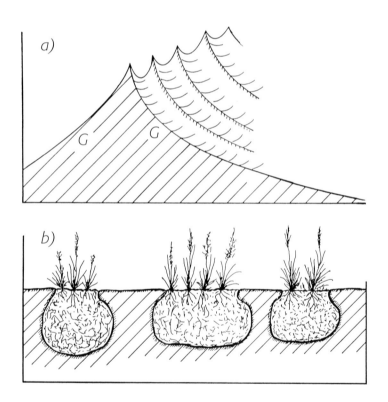

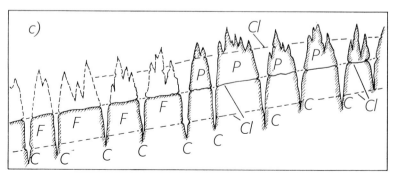

FIG. 70 These drawings show karren stones from karst areas with grooved karren (top), hollow karren (center), and flat and pointed karren (bottom).
(G) Grooved karren
(F) Flat karren
(C) Crack
(P) Pointed karren
(Cl) Clay

48

Stones in this category always have only one hollow or basin, which is filled with soft water. To get a better contrast, we add a drop of milk to the water. Water pool stones are normally displayed in a *suiban* filled with sand.

Be careful! In some of the water pool stones offered for sale, the basins have been made artificially.

Karstic stones

▥ Stones with karren-shaped surfaces
(see Fig. 70)

Here, we distinguish stones with grooved karren, hollow karren (see Fig. 72), and pointed or flat karren (see Fig. 71). They have typical karstic shapes, often resulting in very beautiful stones (see Fig. 75).

▥ Stones shaped like stalactites and stalagmites (see Figs. 73, 74)

True stalactites and stalagmites are not very hard, and they cannot be considered suiseki in the true sense of the word.

▥ Stones in the shape of sinter "curtains"

We often find such shapes in stalactite cavities. They are made of stalactite material, and, therefore, are not appropriate as suiseki. However, among the many different geological formations, we find stones which are very similar to these stalactite "curtains" (see Fig. 76).

FIG. 71 In this landscape stone, we can easily see flat karren shapes in the middle and pointed karren ones on the left. (Collection of W. Benz, 14 inches long, from Ligury, Italy.)

FIG. 72 A hollow karren stone. (Collection of W. Benz, 7⅞ inches long, from Ligury, Italy.)

FIG. 73 The distinct stalactite and stalagmite shapes give a very extraordinary character to this suiseki. (Collection of M. Paiman, 13 inches high, Jakarta.)

FIG. 74 In this suiseki, the missing stalagmites are replaced by the corresponding protuberances of the *daiza*. (Collection of M. Paiman, 13¾ inches high, Jakarta.)

FIG. 75 This bird from Ligury has a surface marked by pointed karren. (Collection of A. Schenone, 7⅞ inches wide, Italy.)

FIG. 76 This curtain-shaped suiseki is clearly indicated by the nearly vertical line structures. (Collection of W. Benz, 8⅝ inches long.)

FIG. 77 This red mountain is located in Monument Valley. Below the steep rock walls lie fallen stone fragments created by erosion. Erosion is a permanent process which nothing can stop.

Erosion mountain stones, similar to those found in Monument Valley

In the Southwest of the United States and in several other regions in the world, "mountains" have been carved by erosion. These shapes have steep sides, and the stone fragments removed by erosion lie at their feet (see Fig. 77). Similar shapes are also found in miniature as suiseki (see Fig. 78). If we look closely at the horizontal layers of the rock base, we understand that erosion must have occurred in several steps.

The erosion pattern shown in Fig. 77 is common in the numerous rock formations of that region. The erosion continues, and in the end probably only solitary sand hills will remain.

FIG. 78 This small suiseki conveys nearly the same impression as the big rock shown in Fig. 77. (Collection G. Benz, 3¾ inches high.)

51

FIG. 80   Suiseki with a "step" erosion profile found in the Ligury region of Italy. (Collection of W. Benz, 25¼ inches long.)

Mountains without peaks, but with a plateau and "step" walls (canyon profile)

The "step" erosion of mountain ranges is not limited to the canyons in the United States (see Fig. 79). We find them wherever there are formations with rock bed layers of different hardnesses.

Such shapes are relatively rare as suiseki. However, we can see an especially beautiful piece in Fig. 80 which comes from a karstic area in Italy.

FIG. 79   From a helicopter at sunset, the "step" erosion profile is obvious. The variety of colors in the different rock beds enhances the effect.

Object Stones
keisho-ishi

These stones suggest objects or subjects found in nature. They have simple, typical shapes. Their line structures immediately remind us of forms that stimulate our imagination.

FIG. 81 The owner found this piece in Bogor in Java. He calls it "Karate." The concentrated strength of the fighter is obvious. (Collection of Hartono, Indonesia, 10¼ inches.)

Human shapes

sugata-ishi/jimbutsu-seki (see Fig. 81)
Suiseki lovers collect stones showing typical human shapes and also those that are very similar to parts of the human body.

For example, Fig. 81 represents a karate fighter, Fig. 82 looks like the head of a lady wearing a hat, Fig. 83 appears to be a monk, Fig. 85 represents a head, and Fig. 86 seems to be a mother with her child.

53

FIG. 82 "Lady with a Hat" was found in China. The shape of the *daiza* is typical for Chinese suiseki. (The stone is 9 inches wide. The photograph was taken during an exhibition in Hong Kong in 1993.)

FIG. 83 This suiseki of a monk (*dusunoki-daruma-ishi*) has been shaped by nature for thousands of years. When we look at this stone, we immediately think of the works of Ernst Barlach. The excellent patina of the stone is especially impressive because it was only created by many decades of exposure to weather. (Stone is 25¼ inches high.)

FIG. 84 The face of this stone only becomes clear with the help of the wooden background. (Stone is 6¼ inches in diameter.)

FIG. 85 This stone, found in Thailand, is shaped like a head. (Collection of W. Benz, 4¾ inches.)

FIG. 87 "The Apostle" is similar to a sculpture by Marino Marini. (Collection of G. Benz, 4¾ inches high.)

FIG. 88 This natural creation could not have been better shaped by Auguste Rodin or Wilhelm Lehmbruck. (Collection of W. Benz, 5⅛ inches high.)

FIG. 86 Object stones suggesting mother and child are appreciated by all suiseki lovers. Christians call these figures "Madonna and Child." (Collection of W. Benz, 7 inches high.)

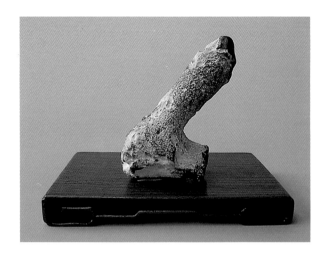

FIG. 89 This flint stone, found on the island of Sylt in Germany, has sexual associations. (Collection of J. Haupt, Germany, 4⅜ inches long.)

FIG. 90 "A Dragon Rises from the Underworld." The dragon is the symbol of good fortune for Chinese emperors. With its dynamic lines and symbols, the elaborate daiza simulates tumultuous water. (Collection of M. Paiman, Jakarta, 13¾ inches high.)

Animal shapes

dobutsu-seki

In this category, we find some animals that come from myths and legends and others that are real or extinct. In any given country, the preferred shapes are those similar to the animals living there. Examples are dragons, tortoises, lizards, Chinese palace lions, elephants, bears, dogs, giraffes, tigers, birds, and fish.

FIG. 91 The male palace lion, a gilded bronze, has a guardian role in the Forbidden City in Beijing. The rather abstract head is typical.

FIG. 92 The upper part of this stone resembles the head of a Chinese palace lion. (Collection of W. Benz, 4⅜ inches high.)

FIG. 93 This stone suggests a large prehistoric proboscidean. (Collection of L.Garbini, Italy, 19¾ inches long.)

FIG. 94 This "poodle" was found in Cirebon on Java. It was a gift from Ismail Saleh, the patron of the In-donesian Bonsai Society and the Indonesian Suiseki Association. (Collection of G. Benz, 4 inches high.)

FIG. 95 A "sitting dog" was found in Bogor on Java. (Collection of N. Kirschten, Luxembourg, 6¼ inches high.)

FIG. 96 This "small bear" was found on the island of Sumatra in Indonesia. (Collection of G. Benz, 3½ inches high.)

FIG. 97 It is not difficult to recognize a rabbit in this stone. (Collection of S. Aziz, Jakarta, 3½ inches high.)

FIG. 98 This "horse's head" is part of the collection created by Mr. Lim Sip Li for the Suzhou garden in Singapore. (Stone is 19¾ inches high.)

Fish shapes

uogata-ishi

Large numbers of suiseki have fish shapes (see Fig. 99). These include perch, dolphin, shark, ray, and catfish. Carplike fish for aquariums are much appreciated in China. Corresponding *daiza* often have very elaborate carvings with wavy structures.

FIG. 99 The photograph of this stone was made shortly after its discovery not far from a lake in Ligury, Italy. (Collection of K. Cressati, Italy, 19¾ inches wide.)

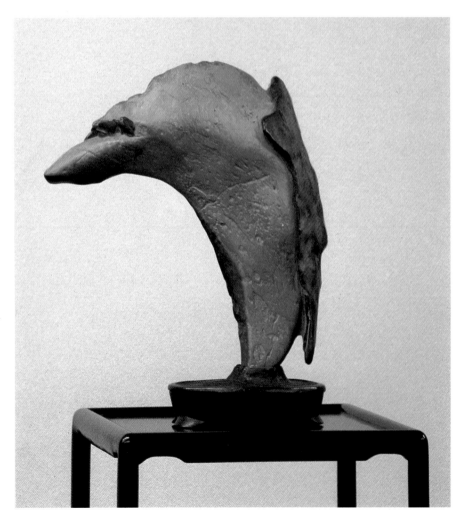

FIG. 101 "A Springing Dolphin" (muroto-tetsug-an-ishi). This suiseki was part of the International Suiseki Exhibition in Tokyo in October 1993. The center of gravity of the stone is relatively high and situated on the left. Its *daiza* has a longer base on the left side to give it the necessary stability. (Stone is 9½ inches high.)

Bird shapes

torigata-ishi (Figs. 102,103)

These stones represent birds, such as the crane (the symbol of long life) or the mythical phoenix (symbol of immortality), but they also represent hens, ducks, geese, birds of prey, and even the phoenix.

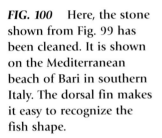

FIG. 100 Here, the stone shown from Fig. 99 has been cleaned. It is shown on the Mediterranean beach of Bari in southern Italy. The dorsal fin makes it easy to recognize the fish shape.

FIG. 102 A hen-shaped suiseki. (Collection of M. Paiman, Jakarta, 9 inches high.)

FIG. 103 Nature has created a beautiful, exotic bird. This stone was found near Bogor in Java. (Collection of M. Paiman, Jakarta, 12½ inches high.)

Insect shapes

mushigata-ishi

In China, insects such as crickets or grasshoppers are sometimes kept as pets. So it is easy to see why crickets, grasshoppers, beetles, dragonflies, and butterflies are especially prized for suiseki in Asia.

House shapes

yagata-ishi (Fig. 104)

Old fishermen's huts, thatched-roof farmhouses (*kuzuya-ishi*), hermitages, and old barns are typical of this type of suiseki. Some stones have a soft calcite vein which tends to be more eroded than the rest (see Fig. 104). This results in a narrow part that gives the stone character.

FIG. 104 This small house is very similar to the thatched-roof houses in the Netherlands, Belgium, and northern Germany. (Collection of W. Benz, 1¾ inches high.)

Bridge shapes

hashi-ishi (Fig. 105)

As indicated by their name, these stones suggest old wooden or stone bridges. They are often presented in a *suiban*. For this purpose, we use a suiseki container with a bluish green glazed bottom to symbolize the water. Then we put sand which matches the color of the stone in the tray so that two separate areas of sand are created. The bridge-shaped stone links these areas. The bluish green river now runs under the bridge.

FIG. 105 This bridge-shaped stone looks like the old bridge of Mostar in Yugoslavia. (Collection of S. Malpeli, Genova.)

Boat shapes

funagata-ishi (Fig. 106)

These stones are very similar to sailboats, rowboats, and Chinese junks. We display them in a *suiban* so that their bows face a large empty space.

FIG. 106 This suiseki looks like a boat. We show it in a marble *suiban* that is too small. Normally, the *suiban* should be two or three times longer than the stone.

Plant shapes and fruit shapes

Many different shapes fit in this category (see Fig. 108). We find, for example, eggplants (see Fig. 107), pears, quinces, apples, persimmons, turnips, trees, and cacti.

FIG. 108 The "bud" on this stone flower is just opening. (Collection of A. Schenone, Italy.)

FIG. 107 We can easily recognize the shape of an eggplant in this typical Chinese suiseki. The photograph was taken during the Suiseki Exhibition in Hong Kong in 1993.

Abstract shapes

(Figs. 109–115)
We often compare these stones to the sculptures of modern artists, such as Barbara Hepworth, Hans Arp, Alexander Archipenko, Constantin Brancusi, and Henry Moore.

FIG. 109 A stone is "born." It seems that the larger stone has given birth to the smaller stone. (Collection of W. Benz, 4⅜ inches long.)

FIG. 110 "Springing Animal." The animal is looking to the left before it springs. The shape of the *daiza* indicates it is Chinese in origin.

FIG. 111 "Winking Genius" is a suiseki from Thailand. (Collection of W. Benz, 9 inches high.)

FIG. 112 An amphora which could not have been better formed by the Greeks. The elegant, two-level daiza shows the amphora to advantage. (Collection of S. Aziz, 5 inches high.)

FIG. 113 "Balance," a suiseki from Thailand, is comparable to a modern sculpture in the cubist style. (Collection of W. Benz, 7½ inches high.)

FIG. 114 "A Weekend Cottage on the Sylt Island" could be the theme of this suiseki, because that is where it was found. (Collection of J. Haupt, Germany, 3⅛ inches high.)

FIG. 115 "Flame" is the name the owner gave to this beautiful suiseki. (Collection of M. Paiman, Jakarta, 15¾ inches high.)

Stones with Striking Surface Patterns

Human Patterns

This category is characterized by mineral deposits representing different types of human beings. In Figs. 116–120, we see some typical examples from a large spectrum of possibilities.

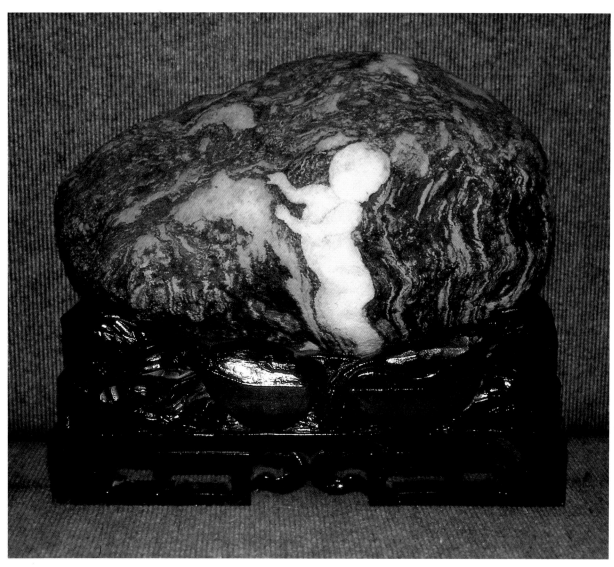

FIG. 116 "A Baby" caught in the stone. (Collection of Rare Stone Museum, Singapore.)

FIG. 117 "Happy Hermit." (Collection of Rare Stone Museum, Singapore.)

FIG. 118 "The Beautiful Tarantella." (Collection of Rare Stone Museum, Singapore.)

FIG. 119 "Lovers on the Beach." A photograph from the second Asia-Pacific Bonsai and Suiseki Exhibition 1993 in Hong Kong.

FIG. 120 "Saint Imploring the Sky." (Collection of Rare Stone Museum, Singapore.)

Animal patterns

This type of stone has surface patterns distinctly showing the bodies of fish (see Fig. 121), birds (Figs. 122, 123), cats, and other animals. Fossil representations, such as ammonites, belemnites, and mussels, do not belong in this category.

FIG. 121   We can easily distinguish a fish in this animal pattern stone. (Collection of Rare Stone Museum, Singapore.)

FIG. 122   A large bird. (Collection of Rare Stone Museum, Singapore.)

FIG. 123   A bird on a stony plant. (Collection of Rare Stone Museum, Singapore.)

Plant patterns

kikumon-seki/kikka-seki/kiku-ishi

Chrysanthemum pattern stones are especially prized. The surface pattern of these stones suggests the radial design of chrysanthemum flowers (see Figs. 124–127). Aside from the flower's intrinsic beauty, the chrysanthemum is a traditional Oriental symbol of immortality. In addition, the sixteen-petal chrysanthemum flower is the crest of the Japanese imperial household. Many Japanese collectors think that the best chrysanthemum stones come from the Neodani area of the Gifu prefecture in Japan. These stones have gray green, wine red, brown, or black colors. They have areas of white or red crystalline stone "flower patterns." Very beautiful stones of this category are also found in the Namhan River in Korea, in southern China, and occasionally in the United States.

FIG. 124 A flower-pattern river pebble from Korea. (Collection of Hartono, Bogor.)

FIG. 125 This river stone with the chrysanthemum pattern was found in southern China. (Collection of W. Benz, 4¾ inches wide.)

FIG. 126 A chrysanthemum-pattern stone with distinct crystals, *neo-kikka-ishi*, photographed at the International Suiseki Exhibition 1993 in Tokyo. (Stone is 9½ inches wide.)

FIG. 127 This beautiful chrysanthemum pattern stone is not a suiseki, but a *biseki*. *Biseki* are cut and polished to enhance their color. (Collection of Bonsai Centrum, Heidelberg, 3⅞ inches high.)

Japanese plum-blossom patterns

baika-seki

The mineral deposits in these stones are similar to the flowers of the Japanese plum tree, which bloom in late winter and are a sign that winter is ending (Fig 128).

FIG. 128 Japanese plum-blossom pattern. (Collection of Rare Stone Museum, Singapore.)

FIG. 129 Grass pattern showing bamboo. (Collection of Rare Stone Museum, Singapore.)

Leaf patterns

hagata-ishi

The mineral deposits in these stones have typical leaf forms. They usually resemble deciduous trees rather than conifers.

Grass patterns

kusagata-ishi

The patterns of these stones resemble mountain grasses, bamboo (see Fig. 129), and other types of grass.

Fruit patterns

migata-ishi

The surface patterns on these stones suggest different types of fruit, such as pears, plums, peaches, pomegranates, and water chestnuts.

FIG. 130 Grass (bamboo) in the wind. (Collection of Rare Stone Museum, Singapore.)

Landscape patterns

Many pattern stones are excellent representations of landscapes (see Figs. 131, 132). I have found stones in this category in the United States, Europe, and Taiwan.

FIG. 131 Fascinating landscape. (Collection of Rare Stone Museum, Singapore.)

FIG. 132 "Mountains with New Snow," a stone from central China. Such stones were used as wall pictures or as furnishings in the house of the Chinese emperor. (Collection of W. Benz, 7½ inches high.)

Celestial patterns

gensho-seki

These mineral deposits have typical forms of celestial bodies, such as the moon (see Fig. 133), the sun (see Fig. 134), and Saturn.

Generally, we distinguish between:

||| Moon patterns
tsukigata-ishi (see Fig. 133)
||| Sun patterns
higata-ishi (see Fig. 134)
||| Star patterns
hoshigata-ishi

FIG. 133 Celestial pattern. We can easily recognize the half moon on the wane. (Collection of Rare Stone Museum, Singapore.)

FIG. 134 Sun partially covered by clouds above a pleasant landscape. (Collection of Rare Stone Museum, Singapore.)

Weather patterns

tenko-seki

The surface patterns represent typical weather conditions which are easy to recognize.

Prized are:
||| Rain patterns
amagata-ishi
||| Snow patterns
yukigata-ishi
||| Lightning patterns
raiko-seki

Abstract patterns

chusho-seki

We frequently find stones with interesting surface patterns. Sometimes, they are similar to tortoise shells, snakeskins, human or animal footprints, or plant leaves.

We distinguish between:
||| Snake patterns
jagure (see Fig. 135)
||| Pit-mark patterns
sudachi
||| Tangled net patterns
itomaki-ishi (see Fig. 136a)
||| Tiger-stripe patterns
tora-ishi (see Fig. 136b)

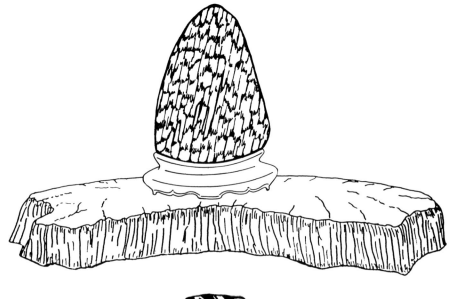

FIG. 136a Drawing of a tangled-net pattern with a *daiza* on a board of sapuko wood *(shizen-ban)*. Sapuko is beautiful, but it is relatively expensive.

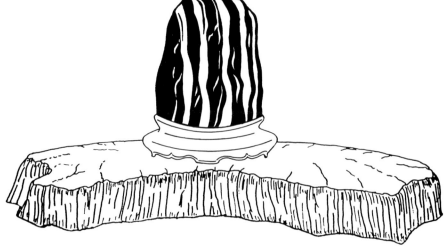

FIG. 136b Tiger-stripe pattern with a *daiza* on a board of sapuko wood *(shizen-ban)*. Sapuko is very hard and has strips along its trunk.

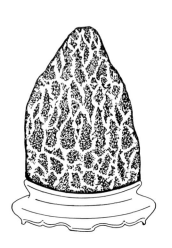

This classification of different surface patterns indicates the patterns most frequently found in stones. Naturally, there are other forms. Surface-pattern stones (*mon-seki* or *mon-yo-seki*) must have clearly visible surface drawings of mineral deposits. In determining the type of stone, the surface pattern is the most important aesthetic element. Moreover, the shape and color of these stones must create a harmonious picture with the surface pattern (see Fig. 137). Then, the suiseki develops an important suggestive power which keeps the observer's attention. Without this feature, a stone is boring and insipid and cannot be classified as a suiseki.

FIG. 137 River stone with abstract pattern, from southern China. (Collection of W. Benz, 7¾ inches high.)

Classification of Suiseki by Place of Origin

Nearly all collectors classify their suiseki by place of origin. Some places have very good stones which are much appreciated by suiseki collectors and command high prices. These places are found all over the world, including Japan, China, and Korea. Stones from these regions are designated by their place of origin, such as *Neodani-kikka-seki,* for example. These are stones from the Gifu region on the Japanese island of Honshu. The map of Japan (see Fig. 138) shows important sites with their names. Stones with no known place of origin are difficult to trace.

Every continent has a number of interesting places to enjoy the personal experience of finding a natural suiseki. Regions of volcanic activity (past or present) are

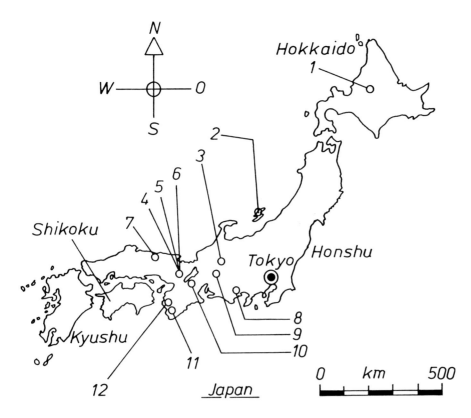

FIG. 138
Map with known suiseki places in Japan.
(1) *Kamuikotan-ishi*
(2) *Sado Akadama-shi* (Sado island)
(3) *Neodani kikka-seki* (Gifu)
(4) *Kibune-ishi* (Kyoto)
(5) *Kurama-ishi* (Kyoto)
(6) *Kamogawa-ishi* (Kyoto)
(7) *Sajigawa-ishi* (Tottori)
(8) *Seigaku-ishi* (Shizuoka)
(9) *Ibigawa-ishi* (Gifu)
(10) *Setagawa-ishi* (Shiga)
(11) *Nachiguro-ishi* (Wakayama)
(12) *Furuya-ishi* (Wakayama)

particularly rich in suiseki. We find stones marked by natural forces, with the ravaged face of time, on the banks of swift streams, in the streambeds themselves, on beaches, in deserts, and in other places where nature has eroded rock.

Here is a description of two sites and their stones.

▌▌▌ Namhan river stones (Korea)

This area is about 62 miles southeast of Seoul. In the riverbed, we find dark gray or black stones. They are beautifully shaped by the sand that the river water transports. Their textures range from fine-grained to perfectly smooth.

▌▌▌ Neodani stones (Gifu, Japan)

Neodani kikka-seki

According to Japanese suiseki lovers, the nicest chrysanthemum stones are found in the Neodani area of the Gifu prefecture (see Figs. 126, 127). The basic colors are grayish green, brown, wine-red, and even black. They have mineral deposits of white or red "flowers."

Classification of Suiseki by Color

Although color represents an essential aesthetic component for some stones (*shikisai-seki*), these stones must also have some degree of suggestive power to be called suiseki.

The attraction of color is that it can symbolize seasons of the year (spring, autumn, etc.) or moments of the day (sunrise, sunset, etc.). Sometimes, we polish the surface of colored stones to enhance their effect.

This method is very similar to the one used by mineral collectors who cut and polish one side of the stone to emphasize what is "inside."

All the classification systems have expanded as we have discovered new stone types over the past few years.

Collecting Suiseki

Minerals and rocks

Geology distinguishes between minerals and rocks. However, because many people confuse the two concepts, we will explain the main differences.

Scientists know of more than two thousand minerals. They consider only about one hundred of them important either because the minerals are common or because they have specific properties. Only two dozen minerals play a role in the formation of rocks. Some names for minerals come from common language, and some others come from the language of mining. There is no single system for naming minerals. International cooperation is necessary in order to standardize the names.

For all suiseki lovers, some criteria are important. These include:
- structure and quality (in Japanese, *shitsu*)
- shape (in Japanese, *katachi*)
- hardness
- color (in Japanese, *iro*)

When we read the different publications on suiseki, we are often confronted with the concept of hardness. For thirty-five years, I have collected and carved minerals and stones. From my experience, I know that suiseki lovers often misuse these terms. Therefore, we'll spend some time discussing these specific terms.

Stones

In ordinary language, we use the word "stone" as a general term for all of the solid parts of the earth's crust. Thus, a mason uses stones to build houses, an engineer uses stones to build a road, and a jeweler thinks of gems and jewels as stones. In the science of geology, however, we speak of minerals and rocks rather than of stones. A rock is an aggregate of several minerals created through a natural process. It is not a homogeneous piece of the earth's crust.

FIG. 141 Mineral collectors appreciate rock crystals like this one. (Collection of W. Benz, 3½ inches high.)

Minerals, Crystals

A mineral is a piece of the earth's crust, created naturally. Minerals are chemically and physically homogeneous bodies which most often have a defined chemical composition. Mineralogy is the branch of science which deals with this subject. Most minerals have definite crystal forms. Crystals (see Fig. 141) have an atomic structure which strictly follows geometric rules. Thus, a crystal is a homogeneous body. The best-known minerals, such as feldspar, quartz, and mica, are the result of a combination of magma and gas from the inner earth and, less frequently, from lava which has reached the earth's surface. Other minerals are created through aqueous solutions, or by the recrystallization of existing minerals, most often under the influence of high temperatures and high pressure.

Crystal forms are important in identifying minerals. Minerals do not always crystallize in regular forms. Sometimes they are distorted because some crystal surfaces develop better than others do. Nevertheless, the angle between the different crystal surfaces is always the same.

Some minerals have different crystal systems. In addition to the outer form, the physical and chemical properties are important.

In addition to the crystal form, we use break, brilliance, hardness, fissionability, and density to identify minerals. The break can be straight, rough, cracked, fibrous, splintery, or mussel-shaped. Brilliance comes from light reflecting on the surface of the mineral. Notice the difference between the brilliance of a diamond, a piece of glass, silk, metal, and grease. Some minerals become opalescent or iridescent.

Sometimes, the minimum hardness (according to Mohs) of a suiseki is justified by the fact that a hard stone is not as susceptible to erosion as a softer stone. But this is only part of the definition. With minerals, hardness also means resistance to scratched. This is the ability to resist being scratched by a sharp instrument. To be able to compare hardness between minerals, the Viennese mineralogist Friedrich Mohs (1771–1839 A.D.) created a hardness scale that has ten levels (see Fig. 142). Unfortunately, his scale isn't linear. Minerals with the same hardness cannot scratch each another. A mineral can only be scratched by one that is harder than it is.

FIG. 142 Mohs Hardness Test. This set contains the "hardness scale," from talc (hardness 1) to corundum (hardness 9). The scale is used by mineralogists.

The method of determining hardness only works with a mineral that has no eroded surfaces. It is not possible to say anything about an absolute hardness using the Mohs test.

Absolute hardness is determined using a method developed by A. Rosiwal. The following table presents the values of Mohs and Rosiwal.

Some minerals exposed to the weather have a deceptively low hardness grade. The hardness grade of some minerals depends on the direction of the scratch.

Mohs hardness scale and Rosiwal's cutting hardness scale

Hardness (Mohs)	Scratching instrument	Cutting hardness (Rosiwal)
1 Talc	scraped by fingernail	0.03
2 Gypsum	scratched by fingernail	1.25
3 Calcite	scratched by copper coin	4.50
4 Fluorite	slightly scratched by penknife	5.00
5 Apatite	barely scratched by penknife	6.50
6 Feldspar	scratched by a steel file	37.00
7 Quartz	scratches window glass	120.00
8 Topaz	scratches quartz slightly	175.00
9 Corundum	scratches topaz slightly	1,000.00
10 Diamond	cannot to be scratched	140,000.00

Normally, we don't use the Mohs hardness test with rocks (most suiseki are rocks) because of the different mineral components.

We also consider another characteristic of minerals and rocks: the "toughness." Anyone who has studied minerals knows that quartz, for instance rock crystal or agate, is a silicium dioxide with a Mohs hardness of 7. This means that both rock crystal and agate possess the same hardness. If we now take two pieces of the same size and try to saw them transversely with a diamond saw disk, we notice that the saw-

FIG. 142 Wind erosion and sandstorms shape rocks in nature. This is what happened to this suiseki, which was photographed at the International Suiseki Exhibition 1993 in Tokyo. (Stone is 6¾ inches long.)

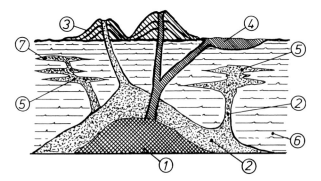

FIG. 144 Different forms of ascending magmas:
(1) magma
(2) magmatite
(3) vulcanite
(4) surface discharge
(5) abyssal rocks
(6) deposits
(7) vein

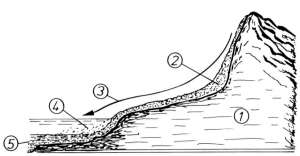

Fig. 145 Creation of sedimentary rocks
(1) initial rock
(2) erosion
(3) transportation of eroded material
(4) deposit of eroded material
(5) consolidation of eroded material
This produces sedimentary rocks.

ing time is different for the rock crystal than for the agate. According to the Mohs scale, both have the same hardness, but they have a different toughness. Agate is tougher than rock crystal.

This feature is significant in the formation of typical suiseki. Tough rocks or minerals are less polished and carved in nature than are softer ones. Nature, in the form of water, cold, heat, wind, and sandstorms, cracks rocks. Because rocks have different components, they are affected by different types of erosion (see Fig. 143).

Rocks

Often called stones, rocks are aggregates of naturally formed minerals. The division between them often occurs after their formation. We can distinguish between magmatites, sediments, and metamorphic rocks.

There are two groups of magmatites. These are formed by red-hot liquid magma (see Fig. 144) in the inner earth

that rises to the earth's surface and coagulates in the earth's crust (formation of coarse-grained plutonite) or is pushed to the earth's surface by volcanic forces (formation of fine-grained vulcanite).

In *plutonites* (granite, syenite, diorite, gabbro, and peridotite), the minerals are mixed together in no particular order, and the visible crystals have no uniform direction. Moreover, they are very compact, have no holes, and are light gray, light green, light brown, and gray black in color. Their density is 2.7–3.3 kg/dm3.

Vulcanites (quartz porphyry, trachyte, porphyrite, basalt, and picrite, with a density of 2.7–3.0 kg/dm3) have a dense mixture; sometimes they are completely amorphous. Only rarely do we find complete crystals. Usually, we observe a direction in the structure. Sometimes we find small holes. Some vulcanites are also prone to acidification. The color ranges from light gray beige to deep black. Between the plutonite and vulcanite group is the group of *gang rocks*, such as granite porphyry, syenite porphyry, and diorite porphyry.

FIG. 146 Basalt mountains appearing out of the morning mist. (Collection of P. Krebs, Germany, 5½ inches long.)

Sediments are secondary rocks (see Fig. 145) formed by erosion and by the deposits of original rocks. Garnet, quartz, and tourmaline are relatively stable against erosion in comparison to feldspar, biotite, and olivine. Through sedimentation (the stratified deposit of eroded material followed by hardening), harder mineral grains are included in softer eroded material.

Sandstone is a typical example. We often recognize sedimentary rocks by their pronounced layer structure.

Metamorphic rocks (changed rocks or crystalline schists) are formed by the transformation (metamorphosis) of any kind of rock under high temperature and/or pressure. As an example, green schist and chlorite schist are formed by gabbro or basalt in the epizone (see Fig. 146); amphibolite is formed in the mesozone; and hornblend gneiss or augite gneiss are formed in the katazone.

The following properties are the criteria for identifying metamorphic rock: full crystalline features with visible crystals, parallel structure (schistose), silk shimmer, very compact, and absolutely no fossil.

Suiseki are primarily rocks, not minerals.

FIG. 147 A volcano in winter. "Pico de Teide" is on the island of Tenerife. At 12,198 feet, it is the highest Spanish mountain.

The following rocks are appropriate for suiseki:

Abyssal rocks (Plutonite)	Gang rocks	Vulcanites
Granite	Granite porphyry	Quartz porphyry
Syenite	Syenite porphyry	Trachyte
Diorite	Diorite porphyry	Porphyrite (andesite)
Gabbro	Gabbro porphyry	Basalt
Peridotite		Picrite

In addition to the rocks mentioned in the table, many other stones make wonderful suiseki, such as gneiss, jasper, petrified wood, jadeite, diopside, serpentine, aktinolithe, chrysoprase, rhodonite, and sodalithe.

Finding Places for Suiseki

You can find suiseki everywhere in the world. However, the best places are those which have experienced or are experiencing volcanic activity (see Fig. 147). Stones carved by natural forces, bearing the ravaged face of time, are found on the banks of swift rivers and streams, in the riverbed itself, in some coastal regions, in karstic areas, deserts, moraine zones, and also places that show evidence of previous erosion. Keep your eyes open and look at the ground. Each region has characteristic shapes and colors.

Equipment for Collecting Suiseki

You can collect suiseki on riverbanks, in streambeds, in abandoned quarries, in rocky forest regions, on mountain slopes, in stone screes, in karstic areas, in desert areas, on sea coasts, and so on. Most of these places are not directly accessible by car, requiring a long trip on foot into a remote place. Be sure to adapt such a trip to your physical ability. You must have the proper equipment, and you must use it carefully.

For personal well-being, you'll find that hiking boots are necessary. For searching in streambeds, you'll want rubber boots. Depending on the weather conditions, you'll need good waterproof and wind-resistant clothing. We recommend a scarf and hat or cap in open country and stone-proof helmets for visits in quarries or steep rock walls.

To collect the suiseki, you'll need working gloves, goggles, a pocket knife, packing material (foam, some form of foam peanuts, or old newspapers), string, a rucksack with a metal frame or a strong workbag, maps, a compass, a notebook and pen, handkerchiefs, a lighter, a viewing pipe for collecting in riverbeds (see Fig. 148), a fist-aid kit, and so on. You'll also want the following tools (see Fig. 149): a geologist's hammer, a small pick (6–8 inches long), a flat chisel (3–5 inches long with a hard metal edge), a pointed chisel, a hammer (1–2 pounds), a small steel garden rake, a small steel brush (see Fig. 157), a small, hard plastic brush, and a small crowbar (19¾ inches long).

For physical comfort, bring along a sufficient quantity of nonalcoholic drinks and easily digestible food that doesn't require preparation. Pack snacks such as apples, dried fruit, and chocolate.

These recommendations should give you some general ideas. They're based on the many trips I've taken. In each new situation, you should decide which equipment is absolutely necessary for safety, but reserve enough transport capacity for any suiseki you find.

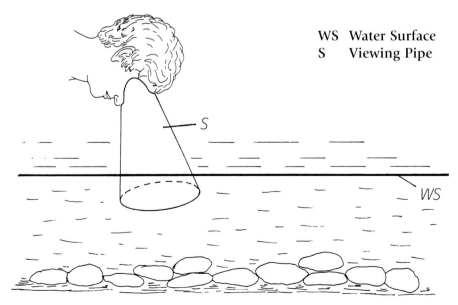

WS Water Surface
S   Viewing Pipe

FIG. 148 Viewing pipe made of opaque plastic to help locate stones in water. The pipe reduces reflections. Just as when we want to window-shop we need to be very near the window and to put our hands against it, a viewing pipe acts to cut down on the reflections which distort the view into the water.

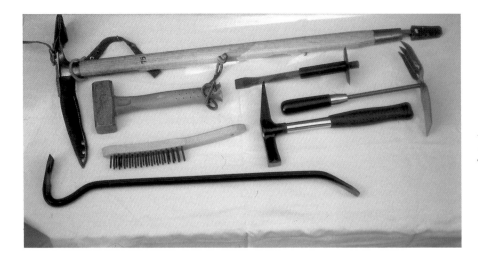

Collecting and Transporting Stones

Many places have easy access and are, therefore, very suitable for stone collecting (see Fig. 150). In order to protect the environment, keep the whole collecting area free of any rubbish. When you leave, everything should look just as it did before you arrived. If you pick up stones from the ground, fill in the holes so that no one can see the area in which you worked. If you lift a stone to observe it, and you realize that it is not appropriate for your collection, return it to the same spot so that it looks as if you had not touched it.

International rules

In addition to public places, there are also private grounds where it is possible to find valuable pieces. To enter these areas, you will need authorization from the owner.

Private grounds are usually indicated by signs or by fences.

FIG. 150 Typical collecting place for stones appropriate for suiseki.

Actually Collecting Suiseki

The following text describes a mental process that often occurs when I collect stones. However, I don't always carry this process through to the end. If a stone is rather difficult to read, it is enough to go through the first five steps to decide whether to keep the stone or not.

1. I find a stone.
2. For some reason, it pleases me.
3. I observe all sides of the stone more precisely (see Figs. 151a, 151b, 151c).
4. I recognize the diversity of colors.
5. I recognize the different shapes on the surface.
6. Is a side especially beautiful, especially expressive?
7. Could this side be the front of a suiseki?
8. Has the shape of the stone a thematic content?
9. Can the stone be classified in a classic group (mountain stone, object stone, etc.) in accordance with its shape?

After you find a stone, you have to protect it. Wrap the stone in cloth or newspaper or use foam peanuts to avoid any damage during transport. Carefully place the wrapped stone in a rucksack or other bag.

FIG. 151a View of the suiseki "Wild Emperor" from the left side.

FIG. 151b The same stone seen from the back.

Use the same care when storing the stone before returning home. Don't allow stones to knock or rub against each other.

At home, be careful when unpacking. Check the stones for small cracks.

FIG. 151c This is the best side of the stone shown in Fig. 151a and 151b. Look at its old face and maturity. The wonderful surface patterns and proportions are impressive.

Collecting Stones in Rivers and Streams

Natural water erosion shapes stones. This erosion process is principally caused by the scraping action of light material and by corrosion. Even hard stones cannot resist the polishing effect of transported or suspended material (grains of sand). These grains of sand are normally on the bottom of riverbeds. Only when the water has enough speed and force are the grains transported. Grains of sand that are 1 mm in size are transported in a river when the water reaches a minimum speed of 8 inches per second. Once the grains are in motion, the speed of the water can decrease without the sand settling to the bottom.

FIG. 152   A waterfall stone with a beautiful polish caused by sand transported in running water.

Only when the water speed falls under 3 inches per second do the grains of sand fall to the bottom.

This means that the desirable polishing action occurs only in rapid waters. Thus, you should only look for stones in places where a significant polishing action is possible. You can estimate the water speed by throwing leaves or small pieces of paper into the water and determining with a stopwatch how long they need to cover a distance of one foot. Experienced collectors do not need to do this. Depending on seasons, stream speed and water height change. For example, September and October are promising collecting months.

As described earlier, in addition to transporting grains of sand, water also carries stones which could well become suiseki. However, the transport speed is very slow and could take hundreds or thousands of years, depending on cir-

cumstances. Sometimes stones are wedged between other stones and remain in the same place for a long time. If we observe the movement of a stone from the upper to the lower part of a river, we notice that the longer the stone is exposed to the polishing action of sand transported by water, the farther along the river it is transported.

Try to discover good collecting sites along the river. For this purpose, examine the same mineral composition in the upper part, in the middle part, and in the lower part of the river. Stones collected in the upper part still have ridges and corners and are not very polished. Stones found in the middle part of the river are rounder because of the polishing effect of the sand. Stones found in the lower part often have a relatively smooth surface (see Fig. 152) because they were polished for a longer period of time.

Because the flow of water is different from river to river, we need to do a test collection in different sections of the river, as described above, unless we already know the river and know where to find beautiful stones. In my experience, when looking at long rivers, the best place is somewhere between the middle and upper parts; for shorter rivers, it is in the middle parts; and for very short rivers, the lower parts. In addition, we need to look for places where the water is running relatively fast.

We also have to remember that in a stream with a slope of 0.2 percent (this means with a gradient of about one inch in three feet), a granite rock only needs to travel about seven miles along the river bed to crumble into ¾-inch pieces. Three or four miles are required for mica schist or gneiss, and only about one mile for soft sandstone. Using these examples, we can estimate intermediate values for other rock types, depending on their hardness and toughness.

Suiseki from Karstic Areas

The term *karst*, which comes from the Slovenian-Croatian mountains near Triest, refers to all the phenomena produced when rock dissolves. Such phenomena appear mostly with limestone, or dolomite. One of the main characteristics of karst is the underground water runoff through splits, vents, and holes. This produces a variety of surface shapes. **Karrens** (see Fig. 70), which are forms of exokarst, are surface shapes of karstification, as are the ones we see in Ligury, Italy, for instance, formed by the dissolving effect of surface water. This produces a large variety of different shapes (see Fig. 153).

Groove karrens or ridge karrens appear on steep slopes. With time, sharp ridges are often formed.

Runoff karrens are formed where water gathers in strong flows. Upper edges are rounded by draining water.

Fissure karrens are formed where surface fissures are present. Water penetrates fissures that are barely visible. The water slowly enlarges the fissures until they become large cracks. With limestone,

FIG. 153 "A Mountain Playing with the Clouds" is a typical Chinese name for a suiseki. (Collection of A. Schenone, Italy, 6 inches long.)

FIG. 154 Small mountain range. (Collection of P. Krebs, 1¾ inches high.)

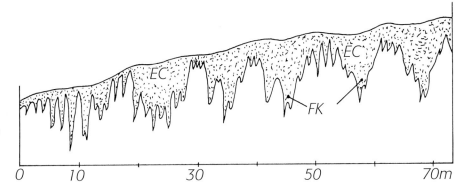

FIG. 155 Geological columns. These are fissure karrens (FK) filled with erosion clay (EC).

FIG. 156a Stone largely covered with erosion clay before cleaning.

FIG. 156b This is the stone in Fig. 156a after cleaning.

large karren areas can be formed, as is the case in some places in Ligury and other karstic regions. With time, cracks can become so deep that different rock layers become separated into segments.

The process begins with runoff karrens, first producing rounded shapes and then, with time, modifying them to pointed karrens. Stones obtained from both runoff karrens and pointed karrens make excellent suiseki (see Figs. 154, 33, 36, 71, 80).

Hollow karrens are formed in open spaces where small vegetation patches that create humus appear on bare karst. These hollow shapes, called *kamenisti*, which range in diameter from ¾ inch–39 inches, are filled with humus (see Fig. 70) and have reflex edges. With time, hollow karrens are modified to cone karstic surfaces.

The cone karstic rock formations resulting from these processes are also appropriate for suiseki. With covered karst, corrosion produces cracks and layered furrows. These formations are called geological columns (see Fig. 155). Erosion clay is more or less present in all karrens, runoffs and cracks (see Figs. 156a, 156b). Sometimes, it is very difficult to remove this clay because it is so thick. It is better to soften erosion clay in soft water containing a washing product before cleaning the stone with hand brushes or steel brushes mounted on a drill machine.

If you're going to use steel brushes to clean a stone, try it in an inconspicuous place first to be sure that you won't damage the stone.

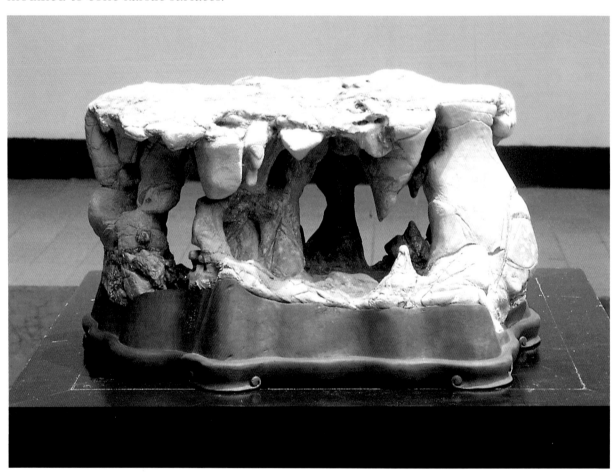

FIG. 157 A typical piece of karstic landscape with stalactites and stalagmites. (Collection of S. Aziz, Jakarta, 11 inches wide.)

Preparing Suiseki

Cleaning Stones

Most stones found in the open have a dirty surface. You should give such stones a first cleaning on the spot. You can do this with wood or bamboo chopsticks, brushes with short and hard bristles, or paintbrushes. If possible, wash the stones in water.

At home, wash the stones with a strong water jet or with a high-pressure cleaner. Then put the stones one by one in a plastic container filled with water. Add several drops of a washing product to the water and mix properly. After five to twenty minutes, examine the stone surface again for dirt and clean with a plastic brush. For very persistent dirt, you may need to soak the stone for several days.

Remove persistent dirt and soft erosion residue with a steel brush, brass brush, or needle brush (see Fig. 158).

A needle brush is easy to make by winding ten to fifteen fine steel needles in a small bamboo tube (used as a haft) with a rubber band so that the needle points stick out about ⅜ inch.

Before using steel brushes to clean stones, test the brush first on an area that won't be visible later—for example, on the bottom of the stone. The cleaning process should not damage the stone.

At the end of the cleaning process, wash the stone again under running water to remove the last remnants of dirt.

FIG. 158 Cleaning tools: (top left to right) small metal hand saws, two spatulas, needle brush, hand brush; (bottom left to right) bamboo sticks, toothbrush, brass brush, hand brush, steel brush.

Cleaning Stones with Wire Brushes

In some cases, a manual cleaning process is not sufficient. For especially persistent dirt, use rotary wire brushes. Steel wire brushes and hard nylon brushes usually produce good results. Both types come in several models with bristles of different hardness (for radial and axial brushes, see Fig. 159a). You can use machine brushes with drills or milling machines.

After starting the machine, experiment by trying the rotary wire brush on several inconspicuous places which you don't plan to display. This experiment will allow you to determine if the surface of the stone will be damaged or not. If the test is successful, you can give the stone a complete mechanical cleaning.

Safety

During the cleaning process, small loose stone pieces and loose bristles may be thrown out. To protect yourself, you need to wear leather working gloves and goggles (see Fig. 159b). You should always clean stones outside. However, even outside, you may need to wear a mask (available in drugstores and specialty shops) because of the dust you are generating as you clean the stone.

The masks come in several styles: ones for coarse dust, ones for fine dust and aerosols, and others for different purposes.

FIG. 159a Electric drills with rotary brushes to clean stones. A hand drill with an axial brush and a stand-mounted drill with a radial brush.

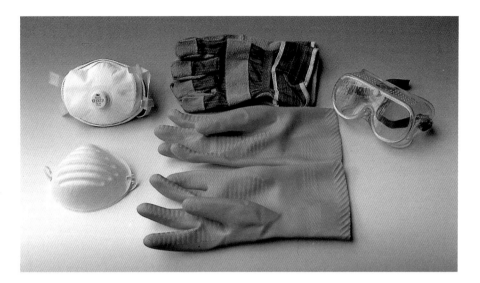

FIG. 159b Masks for protection from fine dust (top left) and coarse dust (bottom left). Leather gloves (top) and rubber gloves (bottom). Goggles used to clean stones with brushes or acid.

You can wear a half mask when working around fine dust (stone and wood dust) and aerosol. You'll find instructions for using the mask on the package.

Even though you'll use a mask, you should do all your cleaning work in the open air or in well-ventilated rooms. If you find that you are experiencing any breathing difficulty, change masks.

Unless you use the mask properly, you won't receive the full benefit. After you put the mask on, check that it is in the correct position. Hold the mask with both hands and exhale forcefully. If air comes out of the sides of the mask, adjust the position and check again. No air should pass through the sides.

Cleaning Stones with Acid

Beautiful stones are sometimes covered with calcareous projections which cannot be removed with a mechanical process. In such cases, you may use concentrated or diluted hydrochloric acid or concentrated formic acid. Be careful with these acids because they are very caustic and poisonous. Follow these instructions exactly:

▮▮▮ Never pour water into concentrated acid (see Fig. 160). The less dense water

will react on the surface of the mixture and splash. Dilute acids by pouring them very slowly into water and mixing at the same time.

Always remember the expression:

"First the water, then the acid, otherwise something dreadful happens."

Be careful not to inhale the inevitable acid vapors. They burn the mucous membranes in the respiratory tract. Do all work with acid in the open air. Wear a mask (found in drugstores and specialty shops). Refer to the preceding section, "Cleaning Stones with Wire Brushes—Safety."

Because acid is very caustic, it will harm your skin and clothes. You must wear good rubber gloves, plastic or rubber overalls, and goggles. Keep plenty of water available to neutralize any spills. If acid splashes into an eye, wash it thoroughly with plenty of water. See an ophthalmologist for medical care.

To apply acid to a stone, use only nonmetallic brushes. Otherwise, the acid will destroy the metallic parts.

After every step in which you've use acid to clean the stone, wash the stone with fresh water to which you've added a cleaning agent.

When you're finished using acid to clean the stone, put the stone in water for several hours. Test the pH level of the water. If the pH level is well below 7, the water is still acidic, and you must neutral-

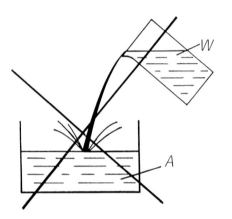
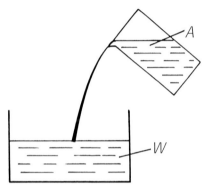

FIG. 160 Diluting an acid. Never pour water (W) into concentrated acid (A). Always slowly pour acid into water, as shown in the picture on the right.

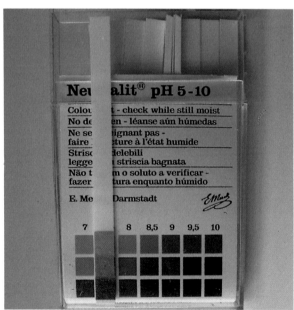

Fig. 161 One test for pH level. You put the test strip into the solution and then compare it to the chart. This yields the pH level.

ize it. The easiest method is to add soda to the water. Pour half a drinking glass of a solution of soda and water into the container and mix thoroughly. Then, test the pH level again. If it is still under 7, add more of the soda solution. Continue with this process until you reach a pH level of 7.

After you've neutralized the acid, allow the stone to remain submerged in water for a while to neutralize any acid which has penetrated the stone's surface.

You can pour neutralized water down a normal drain without any problem. However, disposing of acids must be done correctly. Check the regulations in your area before you start.

One way to test for pH level is to use pH-test strips. You can purchase these strips in drugstores and specialty shops. To determine the pH level, insert the strip into the liquid for thirty seconds to two minutes. Then compare it to the color scale (see Fig. 161) to establish the level.

In case of acid poisoning, obtain medical advice immediately. Many doctors recommend magnesium oxide because it neutralizes acids without forming a gas or attacking membranes.

Drying Stones

After the cleaning process, the stones are wet. We can compare them to sponges saturated with water. Now we must dry the stones.

The simplest but slowest method consists of putting the stones in the sun. Place the stones on an absorbent cloth and turn them over from time to time.

A quicker method consists in drying stones with a hairdryer. Hot air removes water particles on the surface of the stone. After a while, a stone that you dry using this method will become damp again because water comes out of the stone the same way it comes out of a sponge. It only reaches the surface of the stone very slowly.

You can dry damp stones in an oven, but use caution. You'll need to raise the temperature to about 250°F. This has to be accomplished slowly and in several steps to avoid forming vapor bubbles inside the stone, causing it to split. You'll also need to be careful when putting stones in a microwave oven. Try to pre-dry the stone, as you would with the oven method. With microwave ovens, levels of 80 to 150 watts over 15–45 minutes have been tested successfully. Stones treated in this fashion are very hot and prone to break. Therefore, you should put the hot stones on a dry cotton or linen cloth until they are cold.

Obtaining an Even Bottom for a Stone

Many natural stones have uneven bottoms and will not remain upright. Therefore, you have to create a flat bottom. There are several ways to accomplish this.

Working with hammer and burin

First, position the stone so that you can work on it. Sandbags (see Fig. 162a) are appropriate for this purpose. Fill a bag with sand and place it on a stable table. Before you begin working on it, precisely define the position and direction of the bottom. Cover the stone with a second, smaller sandbag. Position a board on top of the second bag. Now, hold the stone, which is between the two bags, in place with clamps (see Fig. 162b). You'll want to use tools such as small burins and hard metal saws.

You must wear goggles and gloves to reduce the danger of injury. In addition, use small, cautious steps in working with the stone.

Working with saws, buff wheels, or stone motor saws

If you can find a stonecutter who has a motor saw, you can flatten the bottom very quickly. Working with a bow saw is a little more difficult and time-consuming (see Fig. 163). You'll need a saw blade designed for hard metal. You can find one in a shop that sells tools. When sawing, water constantly pours into the slot of the saw to maintain the saw's sharp edge. You can also easily produce a flat bottom with a buff wheel. You'll need a specific separating disk on the buff wheel. Regardless of which type of cutting tool you use, be sure that the stone is held in the correct position.

FIG. 162a Sandbags are very good for positioning stones before mechanical work. The sandbag assumes the shape of the stone, giving the stone a stable position.

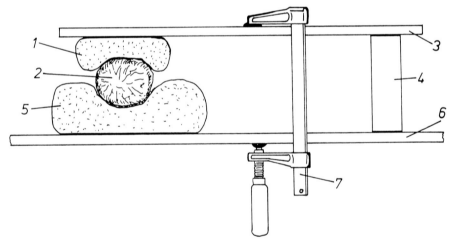

FIG. 162b A stone (2) is fixed with a clamp (7) between two sand bags (1, 5). A board (3) is held in place by a prop (4) at the other end (6).

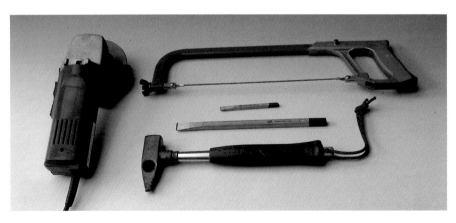

FIG. 163 To get a flat bottom for a stone, use a stone buff wheel (left) or bow saw with a hard metal blade. For more difficult work, use a hard metal burin.

Obtaining a Patina

An ordinary stone needs a beautiful patina to become a suiseki. The silky, mat shimmer of a stone gives it value. You can achieve such a shimmer by rubbing it every day with your hands for a period of thirty to fifty years (see Fig. 83), but that is a somewhat difficult and lengthy process.

A much quicker method for obtaining a patina is to use glycerin, olive oil, or baby oil (see Fig. 164). First, carefully rub the dry stone with one of the products mentioned above. Cover all the splits and cracks in the stone with oil. Then, put the stone in the sun for about three months. Position the stone so that it doesn't get wet from rain or from dew. After this period, rub the stone again with oil and vigorously polish it using a toothbrush, shoe brush, etc. Afterwards, wipe the stone carefully with a clean cloth and then rub it with human body oil from your forehead and hands. After the first treatment, repeat the process, which consists of rubbing with olive oil, brushing, cleaning with a cloth, and treating with your own body oil, every month for a year. After this

FIG. 164   You can give a stone a patina with glycerin or talcum by rubbing the stone according to the directions in the text.

difficult treatment, your suiseki will have a beautiful patina and be ready to exhibit.

Use this treatment with stones that have a smooth surface because you can create the desired silky mat and mystical shimmer on them over a period of time.

Some suiseki collectors who use this process rub their stones with talcum powder and brush them strongly after one or two days. Then they repeat the process every month. Talcum powder is white and oily.

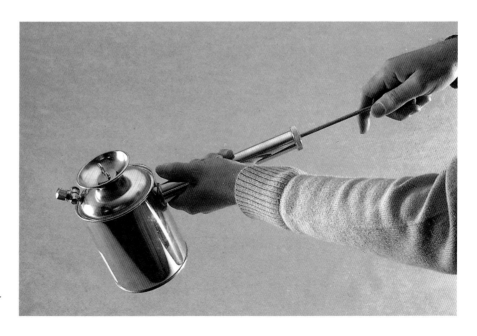

FIG. 165   A water spray. This tool is useful for suiseki and bonsai.

103

Place stones in a container filled with water or spray them with soft water. This means with water that isn't "hard." You can find distilled water in stores, and you may also use ordinary tap water treated with special filters. The local water hardness level can sometimes be obtained from suppliers. Water sprays used for stones are generally the same as those used for bonsai (see Fig. 165). Sprayers such as those used for housekeeping are also appropriate. Place the stones in a shadowy place, for instance under a bonsai bank. In this way, a stone becomes saturated with moisture. After five or six years, the stone has a very natural patina.

Suiseki Care

Once the stone has a patina, you need to maintain it. You should repeat the methods described for dry suiseki in the preceding paragraph quarterly. Suiseki with a patina obtained by spraying water need to be treated regularly. This means you must frequently spray them with soft water. Special "holiday care," which is required for bonsai, is not necessary for suiseki. Suiseki are quite easy to care for. When there is a chance that a suiseki displayed in the garden might get wet and then freeze, cover it with a sheet. If a suiseki gets wet and freezes, the resulting ice could split the stone, causing significant damage. Keep this in mind when you place a suiseki in a *suiban* filled with water. During freezing periods, remove the water from the *suiban*. Better still, turn the container upside down.

FIG. 166   Mountain range in the morning sun. This stone has a natural patina that comes from years of care.

Making a Wooden Base (*Daiza*) to Display Suiseki

General considerations

You can exhibit natural stones as suiseki in different ways.

▌▌▌ Place the stone on a cloth (see Fig. 167), a straw mat, a bamboo mat, a wooden grating, a wooden board (see Fig. 168), or a flat table.

▌▌▌ Place the stone in a ceramic or bronze container filled with water. This was the typical presentation of suiseki in previous generations.

▌▌▌ Place the stone in a ceramic or bronze container filled with sand (see Fig. 169). In Japan, these ceramic containers are called *suiban;* the bronze containers are called *doban.*

▌▌▌ Place the stone on a wooden base (see Fig. 170), more rarely on a stone or bronze base, especially adapted to the stone. These bases for suiseki are called *dai* or *daiza* in Japanese. An artistically elaborate wooden base is called a *daiza.*

FIG. 167 Suiseki on a coarse cloth. The cloth is covered with sand which gives the suiseki extra emphasis.

FIG. 168 Suiseki on an old board. The board is made of teak and has been brushed and waxed. Sometimes, boards from the bottom of boats or from wine barrels are used for this purpose.

FIG. 169 Suiseki in a suiban filled with volcanic sand. (Collection of G. Benz, 17 inches long.)

FIG. 170 A powerful tunnel stone on a *daiza*. (Collection of W. Benz, 14⅛ inches high.)

What is the Role of a *Daiza*?

▎▎▎ It ensures the stability of the stone.

▎▎▎ It presents a static situation and the best side to the observer.

▎▎▎ It may enhance the suggestive power of the stone by completing its shape (see Fig. 171). This requires great artistic skill and technique.

FIG. 171 "Symbol of Masculine" is the name given by the owner to his creation. Notice that the legs of the horse are part of the *daiza*. (Collection of Saleh, Jakarta.)

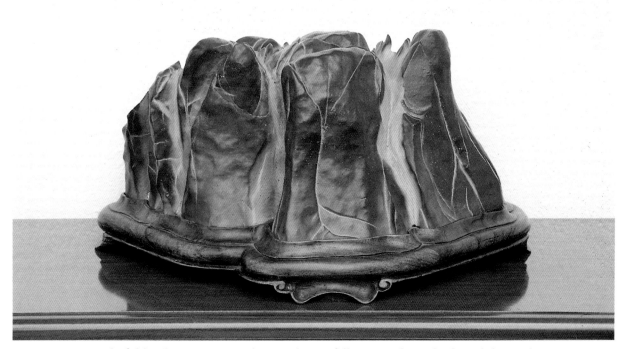

FIG. 172 A wonderful landscape stone with several waterfalls on an elegantly shaped *daiza*. The inconspicuous color allows the stone to show its beauty. (Collection of M. Paiman, Jakarta.)

Sometimes *daiza* are very artistic and strongly reinforce the display value of a suiseki. However, the *daiza* should not compete with the stone. Instead, it must be unobtrusive (see Fig. 172). Before you make a *daiza*, consider the following points.

1. What does the stone suggest? Is it a mountain stone, or an object stone similar to an animal, for example?

2. What is the color of the stone ? What color would be best for the base?

3. Does the stone create a powerful impression or a delicate impression?

4. Has the stone a large bottom or is it rather unstable, top-heavy? Is the stone's bottom even or uneven?

5. Is it necessary to adapt the wooden base to the theme suggested by the stone? Would a wooden base with a corresponding shape enhance the suggestive power of the stone (see Fig. 171)?

FIG. 173 A stone with a very uneven bottom. It was necessary to make a *daiza* which compensates for the unevenness of the stone and, at the same time, puts it in the fore-front. On the left, the half-finished *daiza*.

FIG. 174 The stone shown in Fig. 173 with the finished *daiza*. The front side of the *daiza* is partly open to enhance the sug-gestive power of the stone. I found this stone in Ligury, Italy, and made the *daiza* for it. (Stone is 6¼ inches long, 4¾ inches high.)

Before you decide whether you want to use a *daiza* or a container (*suiban*), you have to answer this list of questions regarding a stone. In other words, the decision must be thought through. In the beginning, a suiseki collector prefers rather simple solutions. But, with time, most collectors require more elaborate solutions. After several years, many collectors find that they want to replace the original *daiza* made for a stone with a better one.

I would like to answer some of the questions posed above and then examine every point in detail.

Question 2. The color of the wood should match the color of the stone. This produces a harmonious effect and places the stone in the forefront for the observer. The waving veins of the wood can increase the suggestive power of the stone when the veins emphasize the outline of the stone. Otherwise, orient the veins lengthwise to give the impression of reducing the width of the *daiza*.

Question 3. The *daiza* must be properly adapted to the stone. Only a narrow split should be visible between the stone and the upper edge of the *daiza*.

Question 4. The height of a *daiza* depends on the shape of the stone. Look for harmony and balance (a sensation of stability and appropriate outline) between the *daiza* and the stone. In gen-eral, the height of a *daiza* should not be more than $\frac{1}{5}$–$\frac{1}{10}$ of the stone's height. For cut stones with an even base, this is easy to achieve.

Question 5. For stones with an uneven base (see Fig. 173), a higher *daiza* is often required to compensate for the uneven character of the stone (see Fig. 174). In such cases, you can identify missing elements of the stone and complete it with a corresponding shape. Otherwise, *daiza* with sides narrowing from top to bottom have a positive effect because they give the impression of being lower.

Questions 3, 4, and 5. *Daiza* have legs. Leg shapes range from very simple to artistically worked. Legs of Chinese *daiza* are sometimes, like the *daiza* itself, very elaborate with richly carved ornaments. The rule is to avoid competition between the stone and its *daiza*.

The number of legs should be uneven (for instance 3, 5, 7, 9), and they should not be placed at regular intervals along the side of the *daiza*. Instead, they should be arranged in such a way that they give a visual impression of stability and balance. A general rule could be that in places where a large mass is visible, place a leg to sustain the weight (see Fig. 174).

Because the mechanical preparation of a *daiza* is not easy, I would like to present a method which, by creating a drawing, is helpful in producing the perfect form.

Central Points—Visual and Material (Center of Gravity)

I differentiate between two central points:

▋▋▋ the visual central point of an object

▋▋▋ the material central point (center of gravity) of the object

Visual central point

This is the apparent center of gravity on a flat picture. The farther away an object is, the flatter it will appear. On a photograph,

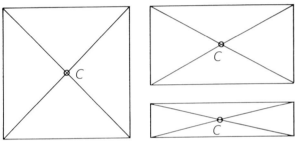

FIG. 175 The center (C) of a regularly shaped flat body is the point where diagonal lines cross.

a three-dimensional object also seems flat. If we want to display a suiseki or bonsai to its best advantage, a knowledge of the visual central point is very important.

How do we find the visual central point of an object ?

For flat objects with regular shapes, such as triangles or squares, draw diagonal lines from the corners. We call these gravity lines. The central point (C) is where these lines cross (see Fig. 175). For a body with an irregular shape, create a flat model using a shadow projection (see Fig. 178). Then, pierce the model with a needle at any point close to its edge (for instance, P1) in such a way that it can freely move (see Fig. 176). Fasten a plumb line to a thread fixed to the needle. This thread indicates the weight line for the hanging point P1. You can draw it on the model with a pencil.

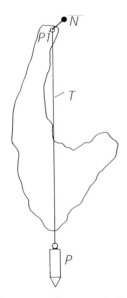

FIG. 176 Defining the first weight line for an irregularly shaped flat body (see text). (N) needle; (T) thread; (P) plumb.

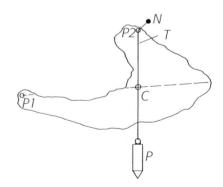

FIG. 177 Defining the second weight line for an irregularly shaped flat body. The visual central point (C) is situated where the weight lines cross.

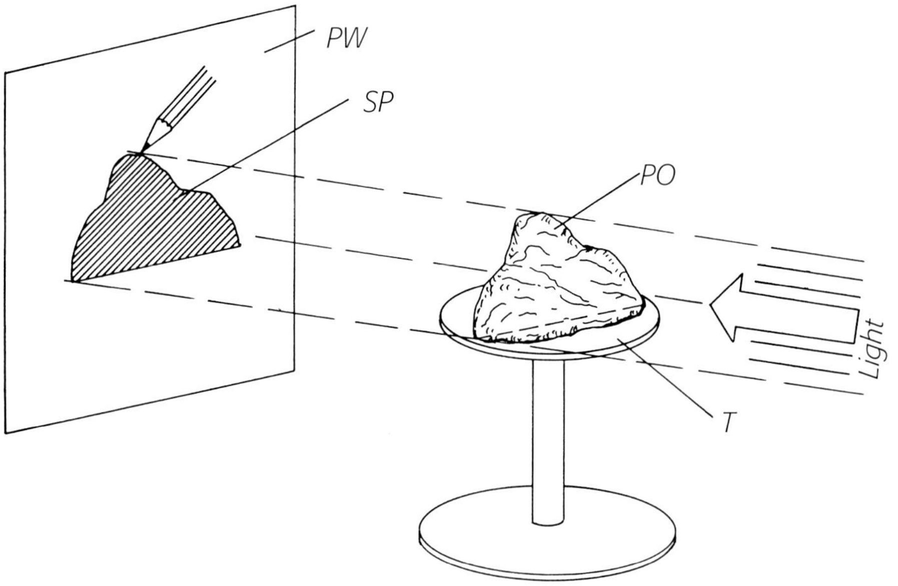

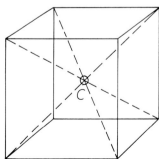

FIG. 178 Example of a shadow projection. The projecting object (PO) is on a table (T). The shadow picture (SP) is created on the projection wall (PW) when the object is illuminated by a distant light.

Repeat the process for another hanging point, "P2" (see Fig. 177). The lines cross at the visual central point "S."

How do we obtain the flat picture of an object ?

We use a shadow projection (see Fig. 178), or we cut out the outline of the object (suiseki or bonsai) from a large photograph.

To produce a shadow projection, we need a projection wall, a thick piece of cardboard, a table for the suiseki, and a slide projector or a powerful light. Place the stone close to the projection wall. Place the source of light far enough from the stone (12–20 feet, if possible). Trace the shadow picture created on the cardboard with a pencil or a pen and cut it out with scissors. The shadow picture has exactly the same size as the projected object (suiseki).

Material central point (center of gravity)

The center of gravity of a body is the point where, theoretically, the whole mass of the stone could be concentrated. For a ball or for a cube, this is the exact center (see Fig. 179). The position of the center of gravity is important for the stability of a suiseki (see Fig. 180). The center of gravity must be inside the limits of the *daiza*, or the stone will fall over (see Fig. 181). To determine the center of gravity, first find the visual center as described above. Then estimate the position of the center of gravity, taking into consideration the thickness of the stone.

Fig. 179 Defining the center of gravity for a cube. This is the point where the diagonal lines cross.

111

For irregular stones, this is a little difficult. After defining the visual center, determine the approximate position of the center of gravity with a stability test. Put the stone on a plate or sandbag, changing its position until the stone is stable.

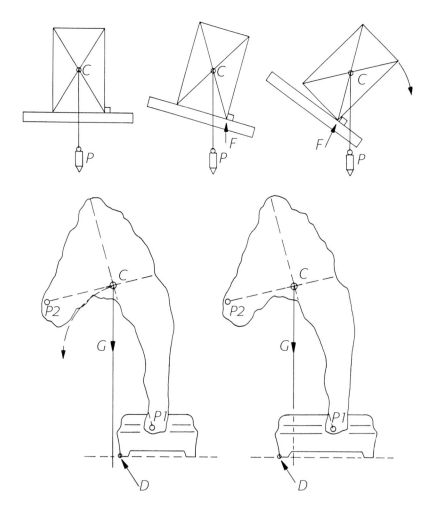

Fig. 180 Stable position of a body (left and center). On the right, the body is falling over because its center of gravity (C) is situated outside the flange (F). "P" is the plumb.

Fig. 181 The center of gravity of a suiseki with a heavy head. In the picture on the left, the *daiza* is too small. The stone is in an unstable position because the center of gravity (C) is situated on the left, outside the edge (D) of the *daiza*. The suiseki falls over on the left side. In the picture on the right, the *daiza* is wider. The center of gravity (C) is situated inside the edge. The stone has a stable position, and the suiseki does not fall down. "G" is the pull of gravity.

Drawing Adjustments for the Wooden Base (*Daiza*) on the Shadow Projection of the Suiseki

We've given different *daiza* profiles in this book (see Figs. 182a–182d).

Here are some indications for selecting the correct *daiza*. In general, the ratio between the height of the stone (suiseki) and the height of the wooden base should range from 5:1–10:1 (see also proportions given in Fig. 188 number 3). This means that the stone should be five to ten times higher than the wooden base. The height ratio depends on the shape of the stone. For a massive stone, a stable and high base is preferred (ratio about 5:1, see Fig. 183). For a slender and elegant stone, a corresponding base with a height ratio of 8:1–10:1 is better.

In addition to the height ratio, the type of profile and the gradient of the outline structure (see Fig. 184) are also important. Vertical outline structures convey an impression of mass and stability; outline structures with narrowing bases convey elegance and delicacy (see Fig. 185).

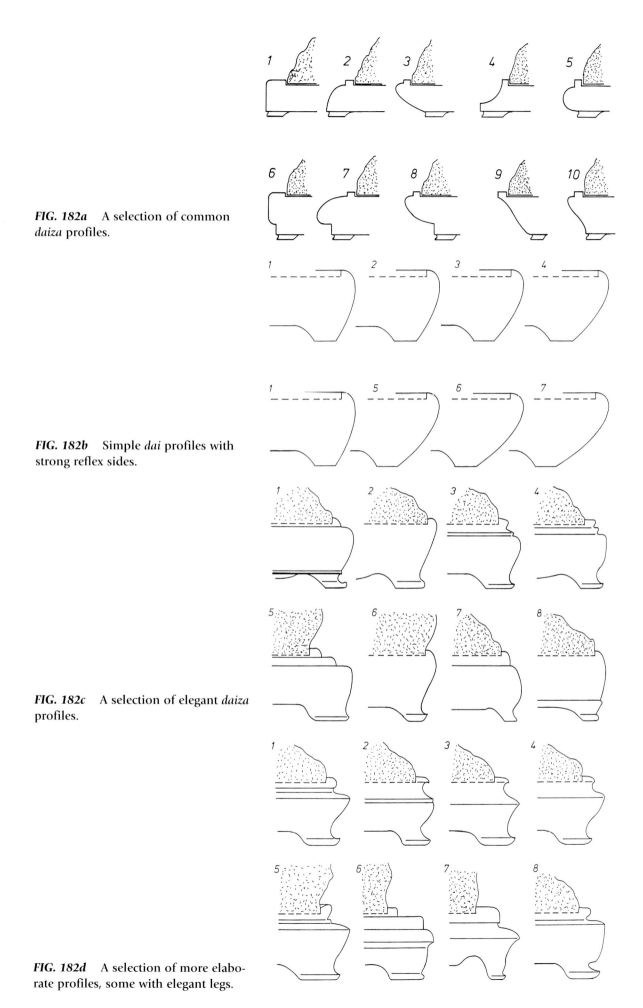

FIG. 182a   A selection of common *daiza* profiles.

FIG. 182b   Simple *dai* profiles with strong reflex sides.

FIG. 182c   A selection of elegant *daiza* profiles.

FIG. 182d   A selection of more elaborate profiles, some with elegant legs.

FIG. 183 A *daiza* with a nearly vertical profile seems heavy.

FIG. 184 This *daiza* with a less vertical profile (compared with Fig. 183) seems more elegant.

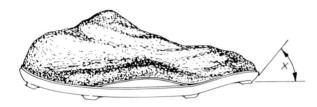

FIG. 185 This *daiza* profile is strongly reflexive. This gives it an elegant aspect.

Which Profile for Which *Daiza*?

There are no strict rules. A feeling of harmony between the stone and the *daiza* should be the deciding factor. The following table gives some general ideas.

Suiseki classification	Appropriate *daiza* profile
landscape stone	
distant mountain	simple, smooth profile (see Fig. 182a numbers 3 and 10, Fig. 182b)
near-view mountain	elaborate, multiple wall profile (see Fig. 182d numbers 6–8)
mountain range with several peaks	simple, smooth profile, one wall (see Fig. 182c numbers 1 and 7)
smooth stone	simple, smooth profile, one wall (see Fig. 182c numbers 1 and 7) Fig. 182d number 4)
thatched-roof hut stone	simple profile with one wall (see Fig. 182c numbers 1 and 7)
suiseki with strong markings	several walls (see Fig. 182c numbers 4 and 5)
powerful suiseki	high, stable *daiza*
suiseki with a large vertical expanse	if odd shape, choose high profile with several walls (see Fig. 186, Fig. 188 number 2)
high smooth stone	simple high profile adapted to the shape at the bottom of the stone (see Fig. 182c numbers 2 and 6; Fig. 188 number 4)

FIG. 186 A powerful sui-seki placed on a *daiza* with an elegant profile, several walls, and elaborate, stable legs.

Sketch of a *Daiza* (Fig. 187)

First, make copies of *daiza* profiles from this book (Figs. 182a–182d), paying particular attention to the height ratio between the stone and the *daiza*.

For the construction, use the example of the profile given in Fig. 182b number 5, with a height ratio of 4½:1. This means that the stone is 4½ times higher than the *daiza*.

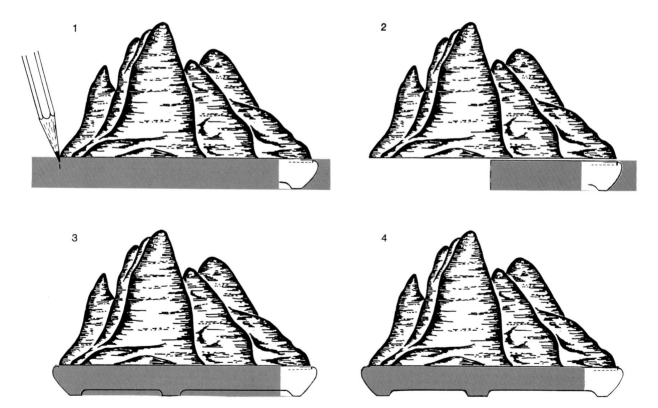

FIG. 187 With the projected shadow of the stone, drawing the *daiza* takes four steps (see text on page 116).

115

First step (Fig. 187 number 1)

First, cut out profile number 5 from the copy and attach it to a paper strip of the same height as the profile. Mark the width of the stone with a pencil on the left side.

Second step (Fig. 187 number 2)

Fold the paper strip to superimpose the left and right marks of the stone. Cut the profiles on both ends and put them under the picture of the stone (Fig. 187 number 3).

Third step

Now, draw the *daiza* legs. Cut out the empty spaces between them. Then put the *daiza* under the "stone." As you can see, this process is useful for all types of suiseki. More than thirty-five different profiles are included, so you'll find a profile for nearly every type of suiseki. Of course, if you are interested, you can develop your own profile, or you can make a *daiza* which reinforces the theme of a particular stone. This is a little more difficult and requires artistic ability.

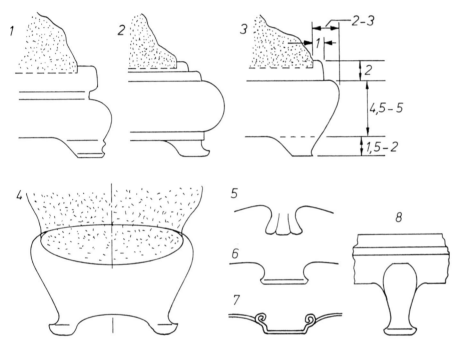

FIG. 188 Two elaborate *daiza* profiles (numbers 1 and 2), proportions of different parts (number 3), and different leg types (numbers 4 through 8). For proportions, the value "1" corresponds to the width of the wall. All other sizes are given accordingly.

In Fig. 188 number 3, you'll see the different size proportions required to design a special *daiza*. The starting value is "1," the width of the wall. The height of the wall is equal to "2," twice its width. The leg height is 1½–2 times higher than the width of the wall "1," and so on. In addition to the suggestions already made to place stones in *suiban* or on *daiza*, you can also use a wooden base with a corresponding profile (see Fig. 189) with a basin filled with sand.

The stone, with its uneven base, is put in the sand. It is very easy to adapt such a wooden base to a stone.

FIG. 189 This *daiza* is actually a wooden *suiban* filled with fine sand, which is used to offset the unevenness of the stone.

Different Types of Legs for Wooden Bases

You'll see some leg types in Fig. 188 numbers 5–8. Other types of *daiza* legs are shown in the profile examples. There are no general rules defining which leg type is more appropriate for a suiseki. *Daiza* legs for powerful stones should have some sta-

bility (see Fig. 190). *Daiza* legs are generally placed where the largest mass of the stone is clearly recognized (see Fig. 191), rather than where a smaller mass is found (see Fig. 192). Legs are never placed regularly.

FIG. 190 *Daiza* for an heavy stone with prominent, stable legs.

FIG. 192 The simple upper edge of this *daiza* is an ideal transition to the simple shape of the stone, but the legs freely express a fantasy.

FIG. 191 Powerful waterfall stone with elaborate, stable legs.

Different Types of Wood for *Daiza*

For suiseki, we prefer wood without marked grains. Appropriate wood types are maple, apple, birch, pear, beech, oak, ash, persimmon, cherry, larch, lime, mahogany, walnut, poplar, Brazilian rosewood, and teak. Soft and hard woods are both used to make *daiza*. Regional availability defines which wood will be used. In Korea, the veins of strongly grained wood are part of the artistry of *daiza* making.

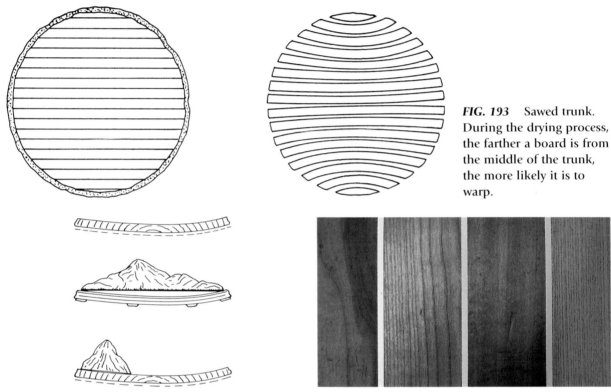

FIG. 193 Sawed trunk. During the drying process, the farther a board is from the middle of the trunk, the more likely it is to warp.

FIG. 194 With very long daiza, the wood's grain must also run lengthwise. If this is not the case, warping will create an empty space between the stone and the *daiza* (see picture in the center).

FIG. 195 Examples of different woods used to make *daiza*. From left to right: plum, cherry, lime, and elm.

Wooden boards for *daiza* come from tree trunks (see Fig. 193). During the drying process, newly cut boards tend to warp if they are not stored properly. As we can see in the picture, the boards from the middle of the trunk don't warp very much. However, the boards from the outer part of the trunk are much more inclined to warp. In fact, the farther the board is from the middle of the trunk, the more likely it is to warp. Be sure to take this characteristic into account when choosing the material. If you select a board with veins that are oriented lengthwise, then there is no real risk of a change in the shape of the *daiza* with time. Otherwise, there is a risk that the finished *daiza* will warp (see Fig. 194). Warped wood creates an empty space between the *daiza* and the stone.

Wood must be stored long enough to dry properly. Sometimes this takes ten years. Green wood warps with time, its shape changes, and unsightly cracks form. You must take these characteristics of the wood into consideration, or you may find that you have made a *daiza* that, in time, won't be useable. Not all woods warp in the same way. The following table gives some indications for different types of wood (see Fig. 195).

Characteristics of Different Types of Wood

Type of wood	Color	Hardness	Warping	Features
acacia (*Bauhinia...*)	black	hard	minor	very heavy, fine pores
alder (*Alnus...*)	whitish, reddish	medium	medium	light, large pores
apple (*Malus...*)	brown, light red	medium	minor	harder than maple, large pores
ash (*Fraxinus...*)	whitish yellow, brown, yearly rings	hard	medium	large pores, very tough, solid, medium weight, elastic
beech (*Fagus sylvatica...*)	reddish, red brown	hard	stiff	solid, coarse, durable
box (*Buxus...*)	yellow, yellowish	very hard	minor	large pores, strong, durable
cherry (*Prunus...*)	red, red brown, red yellow	hard	minor	medium weight, large pores
elm (*Ulmus...*)	reddish brown	medium	medium	coarse pores, tough, medium weight
fir (*Abies...*)	light yellow, shiny	soft	minor	almost no resin, light
holly (*Ilex...*)	whitish, yellowish green	hard	strong	large pores, tough, elastic
ironwood (*Casuarina...*)	red brown	very hard	minor	hard to work on
larch (*Larix....*)	yellow red, shiny	soft	medium	coarse pores, light
lime (*Tilia...*)	reddish white	soft	minor	elastic, good to carve
locust (*Robinia...*)	greenish yellow	very hard	medium	elastic
mahogany (*Swietenia...*)	brown red, yellow red	hard	minor	large pores, good to polish
maple (*Acer platanoides, Acer pseudoplatanus*)	whitish, shiny	soft	minor	elastic, fine pores, fairly heavy, good to polish
oak (*Quercus...*)	yellow, yellow brown	hard	minor durable	hard, large pores,
olive (*Olea...*)	yellowish, leathery color	hard	minor	hard, fine pores
pear (*Pirus communis*)	reddish, red brown	medium hard	medium	heavy, fine pores, durable
pine (*Pinus silvestris...*)	yellow red, reddish brown	soft	minor	light, coarse, a lot of resin
pitch pine (*Pinus regida*)	yellow, reddish	medium hard	minor	a lot of resin, red year rings
plum (*Prunus...*)	red, red brown, blue red	hard	minor	moderate weight
poplar (*Populus...*)	white, yellowish white	soft	minor	light, good to carve
rose (*Rosa*)	yellow, brown red	hard	minor	hard
rosewood (*Jaracanda...*)	dark red brown	hard	medium	large pores, good to polish
service tree (*Sorbus torm.*)	leathery yellow, red brown	hard	minor	fine pores, hard
teak (*Tectona grandis*)	light brown, reddish brown	hard	medium	heavy
thuja (*Thuja*)	dark reddish brown, gray	soft	medium	light, beautiful grain
walnut (*Juglans...*)	reddish brown	medium hard	strong	large pores, good to polish
yew (*Taxus...*)	yellow, yellow brown	medium	medium	beautiful grain

Grain and Surface Treatment of Wood

Type of wood	Grain	Surface treatment
ash (*Fraxinus...*)	pronounced, distinctive markings	polish, varnish, wax
beech (*Fagus...*)	straight lines with small brown stripes, yearly rings hardly visible	varnish, glaze
birch (*Betula...*)	straight stripes on light background	polish, mat, varnish
cherry (*Prunus...*)	very grainy, yearly rings clearly visible	polish, varnish, wax
elm (*Ulmus...*)	yearly rings clearly visible, very grainy	polish, varnish, wax
larch (*Larix...*)	regular, even grain; large yearly rings clearly visible	varnish, wax, oil
lime (*Tilia...*)	very grainy	polish, varnish, mat
mahogany (*Swietenia...*)	large variations, including spots, waves, stripes, and mottles	polish, varnish, wax
maple (*Acer platanoides*)	straight lines, yearly rings visible, often wavy with "bird's eyes"	polish, mat, varnish
oak (*Quercus...*)	pores clearly marked, straight lines, veins visible as straight lines	wax, glaze
pear (*Pirus...*)	straight stripes on light background	polish, mat, varnish, wax
pine (*Pinus...*)	dark stripes, yearly rings on light background	varnish, wax, oil
plum (*Prunus...*)	very grainy, fine pores	polish, varnish, wax
rosewood (*Jacaranda...*)	very grainy, grain clearly visible	polish, varnish, wax
spruce (*Picea...*)	regular, even grains; clearly visible yearly rings	varnish, wax, oil
walnut (*Juglans...*)	dark stripes, very grainy, pores clearly visible	polish, varnish, wax
yew (*Taxus...*)	vivid, yellowish to reddish	polish, varnish, wax

Making a Wooden Base (*Daiza*) for a Suiseki

First step

Put the bottom of the stone on the piece of wood you are planning to use as the base. Mark the outline of the stone on the wood (see Fig. 196) with a pencil (do not use a felt-tip or ballpoint pen). Then draw a second outline approximately $1/16$–$3/8$ inch larger than the first outline (see Fig. 197).

Second step

With a knife or chisel, carve out a cavity inside the smaller outline. The stone will sit in this space (see Fig. 198). The depth of the depression depends on the shape of the stone. For stones with an even bottom, $1/32$–$1/16$ inch is enough. For uneven stones, you have to adapt the depth to the unevenness of the base. Begin by rubbing the bottom of the stone with chalk and pressing the stone into the cavity.

FIG. 196 Draw the outline of the stone on the wood with a pencil.

FIG. 197 Draw a second outline contour about 1/16 inch away from the stone.

Where the cavity is not deep enough, you'll find chalk on the wood. That makes it easy to see where you need to remove more wood. Repeat this process until the stone is perfectly adapted to the desired depth in the wood. Instead of knives or chisels, you can also use a milling machine or other multipurpose tool which you can adapt for this job. These machines should have speeds of over 20,000 rotations per minute. Milling cutters must be made of hard metal and have appropriate profiles.

Before starting to mill the wood, cover the blades with a wax film by touching them to a block of paraffin or to a wax candle. This will coat the blades so that the shavings will not stick to them. In this way, the milling cutter stays sharp longer. From time to time, repeat this waxing process.

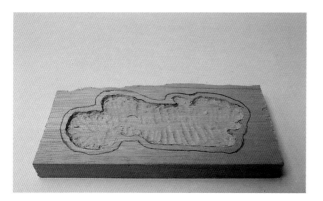

Fig. 198 Cut a cavity for the stone with a knife. Be careful to avoid leaving large, empty spaces near the outline.

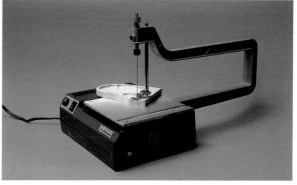

Fig. 199 With a jigsaw or fretsaw (as in this picture), cut the daiza along the second outline.

Third step

When the cavity is finished, cut the wooden base along the second outline with a jigsaw or fretsaw (see Fig. 199).

Remove any irregularities at this point so that you can mill the stone's profile properly.

Fourth step

Now, you need to cut along the second outline, using wooden files and mill cutters. This step requires some skill. You should practice on easy profiles before you tackle more complicated ones.

121

FIG. 200 Once you've made the outline and the legs, the *daiza* begins to take shape.

FIG. 201 Bow saw (on the left), a file, different groove and hollow chisels, carving knives, and a brush (on the right).

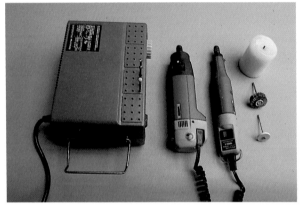

FIG. 202 Electric milling machines (center), transformer (left), candle, emery and grind heads (right).

FIG. 203 Emery heads (center and right) and grind heads for electric milling machines.

Once you've carved or milled the outer outline (see Fig. 200), polish the surface carefully with fine sandpaper.

To increase its efficiency and durability, rub the sandpaper on its smooth side (not the polishing one) against the edge of a table or board before starting the work. Always polish wood with longitudinal grains in the direction of the veins. For other types of grains, use a circular movement. Always start the polishing process with coarse sandpaper, change to a less coarse grade, and finish with a fine grain.

FIG. 204 Set of grinders. Grinders of hard metal are good because they stay sharp longer.

FIG. 205 Set of tools for polishing with cotton, rubber, and felt.

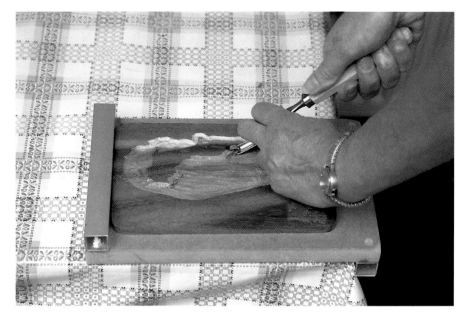

FIG. 206 A practical tool for holding the wood while carving is easy to make. Use a board with wooden laths or aluminum rectangular tubes (as in the picture) at both ends. The aluminum on the right side of the tube holds the board at the edge of the table. Place the future *daiza* on the board and hold it in place with the aluminum tube on the left.

As soon as the sandpaper loses its efficiency, replace it with a new sheet. Brush the wood dust away frequently. Use fine steel wool for the final finish. Polish with care because the polish is what the viewer sees.

An old craftsman's proverb says:

"A good finish is half polish."

At the end of the process, wipe the wooden base with a wet rag. This causes the small wood fibers to stand up, and the surface is coarse again. Finally, rub the surface carefully with fine sandpaper or steel wool. The surface is now really smooth.

You can find appropriate tools for woodworking in specialty stores (see Figs. 201–206).

Fifth step

After carving the legs on the underside of the wooden base, you can begin to dye the wood.

Dyeing modifies the color through a chemical reaction that occurs between the chemical and the tannin in the wood. This doesn't change the natural appearance of the structure. When dyeing wood with little tannin, you'll need to use a pre-dyeing product before you begin the dyeing process itself.

In addition to the chemical dyeing process, you can use another process that simply stains the wood. With this method, you apply only a thin layer of color to the surface of the wood.

For chemical pre-dyeing, use the following products:

for yellowish brown colors	tannin
for brown colors	pyrogallus acid
for gray colors	gallus acid
for reddish brown colors	catechu
for purple to black colors	bluewood extract

You can create intermediate colors by mixing the products.

▌▌▌ Rub the wood with a pre-dyeing product and let dry about twenty-four hours.

▌▌▌ Apply the dye lightly with a brush or sponge in the direction of the grain. The dye must also dry for twenty-four hours. Before you begin, try both products on a area that won't be seen.

Sixth step

Wood matting, lacquering, varnishing, and waxing

For matting, use nitrous or shellac matting products. First, treat the wood with a diluted hardening product. Once the wooden surface is dry, polish it again with steel wool and apply matting with a cotton ball. Matting leaves the pores open.

For lacquering, you'll also need to treat the wood with a hardening product. Once the surface is dry, polish it with steel wool and use a brush to apply a colorless lacquer in the direction of the grain.

For varnishing, treat the wood with a "pore filler" first. Then apply the varnish (shellac varnish, nitrous varnish, etc.) with a cotton ball. Nitrous varnish is easy to use. You'll need a dry, warm room for varnishing.

Use light pressure to apply shellac varnish in the direction of the grain. Use regular and quick strokes with a clean cotton ball until you have a silky shimmer.

You should only wax wood with high-quality beeswax, natural turpentine oil, or carnauba wax. Apply the wax lightly and regularly with a soft cotton cloth after you've dyed the wood and polished it again with fine steel wool. After allowing it to dry for about an hour, you can rub the surface with a clean cloth. This produces a silky shimmer (see Fig. 207).

You can use different kinds of wax available in specialty stores, or you can use beeswax from an apiarist.

Use only high-quality wood stains. This is ideal for a first treatment and is also appropriate to renew altered *daiza* surfaces. Before use, shake the bottle or container properly to mix the color pigments thoroughly.

FIG. 207 The *daiza* is now ready. It has been polished with fine sandpaper and then waxed.

In the first treatment, brush the wood with an undiluted stain once, twice, three times, or more, according to the desired color intensity. The surface must be clean, dry, and not oily. Apply the glaze lightly with a soft, wide brush, first crosswise and then lengthwise in the direction of the grain. To renew an "old" surface, clean thoroughly with a turpentine substitute first. Then polish with very fine sandpaper and brush away any dust. Treat the surface with the glaze in the same manner as described above.

You can mix different colors of wood glaze from the same manufacturer in order to obtain any desired color.

Elements for Suiseki Display
Containers, Trays, Sand

Very flat watertight containers or trays (*suiban*—ceramic, or *doban*—bronze) with shallow rims (¼–¾ inch) are very good for displaying suiseki (see Fig. 208). Generally, we fill them with sifted sand (with a grain size of about ¹⁄₁₆ inch or less) or water or both. A tray filled with sand symbolizes a large plain or an ocean or even, possibly, a large crowd, depending on the type of stone. A tray filled with water or water and sand always symbolizes a large stretch of water.

To suggest a large plain or stretch of water, the tray should be two or three times longer that the stone (see Fig. 25).

You should position the stone asymmetrically, so that its visual central point is in a position defined by the golden section (see "Golden Section").

The steep slope of the stone faces the outer side (smaller distance to the edge), while its gentler slope (the direction of movement) faces the vast plain.

FIG. 208 Suiseki in a *doban* (bronze tray) filled with white sand. This type of *suiban* is made in Korea. (Collection of P. Adijuwono, Jakarta.)

FIG. 209 Place the visual central point of the stone above the golden section of the container.

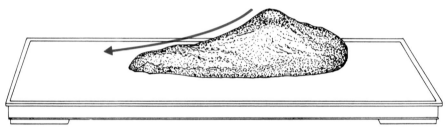

FIG. 210 A typical ceramic container (suiban) for displaying suiseki. (The ceramist is Peter Krebs of Germany.)

FIG. 211 *Doban* (bronze tray) with the typical patina of old containers. This one was made in Japan.

Put in such a position, the stone in the container (*suiban*) presents a harmonious picture (see Fig. 209).

The sand is washed quartz sand with grains of the same size, color, and grit as different sorts of stones, such as yellow porphyry, dark basalt, and gabbro. Also with grains of the same size and color, you might use poroton (average brown) and different sorts of bird sand, black volcanic sand, such as the type found in San Marko bay on the island of Tenerife.

The colors of the stone, the container, and the sand must match (see use of the color wheel, Fig. 238).

Do not fill containers with water or sand to the top. Fill only about 80 percent and leave the remainder empty.

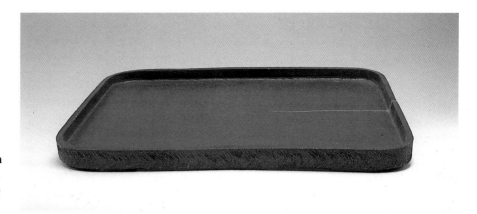

FIG. 212 Suiban with a crack (on the right) which has been "ennobled" with gold by a goldsmith. (The ceramist is Peter Krebs.)

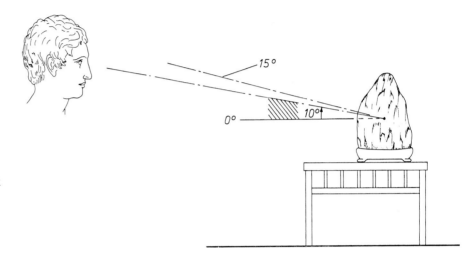

FIG. 213 Suiseki on *daiza* should be viewed at an angle of 0–20 degrees to capture the suggestive power of the stone correctly.

Some *suiban* have a colored glazed bottom. By leaving some surface free of sand, this bottom can be part of the display,

Suiban are made of ceramic (see Fig. 210); *doban* are made of bronze. Bronze containers are very expensive but they are also very beautiful because of the color of the natural patina. Bronze containers generally have ornamental sides; most ceramic trays have plain sides (see Fig. 211). All containers have oval or rectangular shapes; they are very rarely round. When choosing a *suiban*, keep in mind that a "noble" stone requires a "noble" *suiban*. The value of a suiseki can be considerably increased by the careful choice of a *suiban* matching in color, glaze, and texture. If you have the opportunity to work with a good ceramist, he or she can adapt a *suiban* specifically for your suiseki. This is

the ideal case. Otherwise, you may want to take your stone to a shop that sells containers and try to find the best possible combination of *suiban* and stone. In addition to color, glaze, and texture, you'll need to consider the container shape and size, as well as the side height and leg types. The combination of *suiban* and suiseki must represent a harmonious whole. Depending on the sort of clay used to make them, large containers may have a tendency to crack. This must not be seen as bad luck. A good goldsmith can fill the crack with gold (see Fig. 212). The gold makes it watertight again and creates a very interesting artistic result. This can be expensive. In fact, it increases the value of a *suiban* tremendously, especially if the filled crack remains clearly visible in the display.

When you display or exhibit a suiseki in a *suiban*, it should be on a stand, table, or in a *tokonoma* below eye level so that the observer sees the expanse of the plain or ocean inside the container. If the suiseki is not in the proper position relative to eye level, the whole symbol of the display is lost.

In fact, I have noticed that suiseki with *daiza* are often placed in a position that is too low, and this happens in Asian countries, too. A bonsai table with long legs is not sufficient to place a suiseki at eye level, but it is a better position for the observer than some other choices. Suiseki should be observed at an angle of 10–20 degrees (see Fig. 213).

In addition to the different suiseki displays mentioned before, another possibility, rarely used, consists of placing the suiseki in a tray covered with different types of dwarf moss, as seen in Japanese moss gardens.

As a variation, the bottom of the container is partly covered with moss, and the rest is filled with sand matching the color of the moss.

Sizes of Bronze and Ceramic Containers (*Suiban/Doban*)

Suiban (ceramic) and *doban* (bronze) are watertight containers for displaying suiseki. The heights include the legs (see Fig. 214).

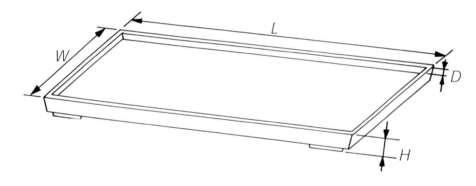

FIG. 214 Indications for sizes of rectangular *suiban*. For oval *suiban*, sizes are also given with the length (L), the width (W), and the height (H).

▮▮▮ Ceramic containers (*suiban*)—
all dimensions are in inches

Rectangular shape			Oval shape		
length	width	height	length	width	height
15¾	9	1	6¾	4	¾
18	11	1¼–1½	13¾	9	1
19¾	10¾	1¼–1½	17¾	10¾–11¾	1¼
20¾	11½	1¼–1½	19¾	11¾–12½	1¼
22¾	10¾	1¼–1½	21¾	12½	1¼–1½
23¾	9–12½	1¼–2	23¾	15–16½	1¼–1½
25¼	7¾–13¾	1¼–2	25½	14½	1½–2
28	9¾–15¾	1½–2¾	28	15¾	1½–2
31½	11¾	2–2¼	29½	17¾–18¾	1½–2
33½	13¾–17¾	2–2¼	31½	18½	1½
35½	13¾	2¾	33½	19¾	2¼–2¾

▌▌▌ Bronze containers (*doban*)—

all dimensions are in inches

Rectangular shape			Oval shape		
length	width	height	length	width	height
11¾	7¾	1¼	11¾	7	1¼
15¾	7–8½	¾–1	13¾	8½	¾
17¾	7–11	¾–1¼	17¾	9	¾–1¼
19¾	10¼	1½	19¾	8½–12½	1¼
21¾	11¾–13¾	1¼–1½	21¾	13¾	1¼
23¾	13	1½	23¾	15	1¼
29½	16½–20½	1½–2¼	29½	17¾–18½	1½
31½	18¾	2¼–2¾	31½	17¾–19¾	2¼–2¾

Legs are ³⁄₁₆–¾ inch high. When choosing a container (*suiban* or *doban*), the ratio between stone height and side height should be 4:1–10:1. This means that the stone is 4–10 times higher than the side.

For lengths, the ratio should be 2:1–2½:1.

If you are going to place the container on a table or stand, then the ratio between the height of the table and the suiseki should be 2:1–8:1. This means that the table is 2–8 times higher than the suiseki. The length of the table depends on the length of the container.

Ideally, the ratio of lengths 1½:1–2:1 (see Fig. 215).

If you place the container on a straw mat or a board, the mat or board should be at least 15–30 percent larger than the container.

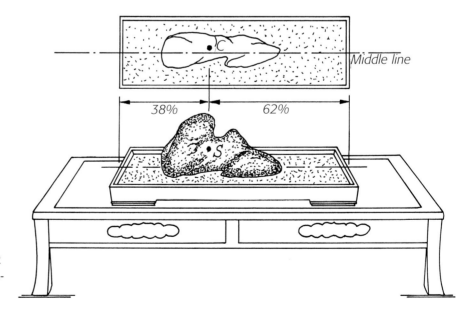

FIG. 215 The choice of the table depends on the length of the container. The table should be 1½–2 times longer than the container.

Mats, Stands, and Tables to Display Suiseki

Which mats or stands are used to display suiseki?

In old China, people placed wool cloth with the typical Chinese red color on tables or shelves to display suiseki. They also used white, green, dark blue, or brown wool cloth. When using cloth, select the color that best matches the suiseki according to the color wheel.

Tatami mats (rice straw mats) and woven bamboo mats (*take-dai*) are neutral in color. Coarse linen cloth or jute is also good to use. In addition to cloth, light-colored sifted sand is sometimes used.

Sprinkled on the cloth, it defines a surface, often with irregular contours. This helps focus the observer's attention on the object.

When using a low table in Asian style, raise the suiseki above its surroundings. This gives the impression it is something particularly valuable. These tables are called *shoku* or *taku*. They can be made of either simple boards or precious wood. The size of the table depends on the size of the tray (see "Containers, Trays, Sand").

FIG. 216 A Chinese *kitaku* with a suiseki. (Collection of M. Pauli, Bern, Switzerland.)

FIG. 217 A suiseki on a Japanese *chu-taku*. The suiseki has the shape of a high plateau with typical flat karren. (The stone is 5½ inches wide.)

FIG. 218 The coin placed next to the miniature mountain on this *maki-dai* defines the scale. (Collection of W. Benz, 1 inch high.)

Different Types of Tables, Stands, and Wooden Boards

kitaku	low table, 4¾–5½ inches high, curved sides and legs (see Fig. 216)
chu-taku	similar to *kitaku*, but only about 4 inches high (see Figs. 217, 219a)
kitaru or *fumi-zuku-e*	long, low table with legs that angle outward (see Fig. 215), legs maintained by a brace in the upper third
hira-taku	very low table, only ¾–1½ inches high, often with rolled legs (see Fig. 219d)

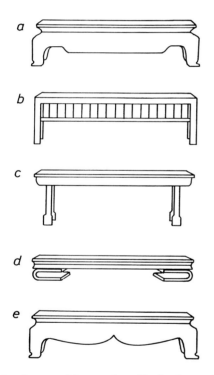

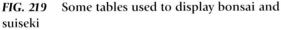

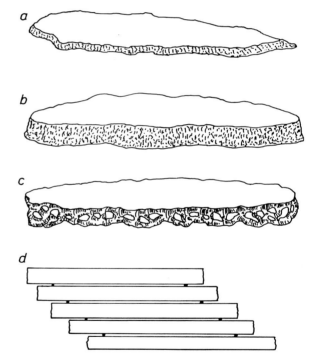

FIG. 219 Some tables used to display bonsai and suiseki
a) *chu-taku*
b) and c) medium-sized tables
d) *hira-dai*—a very low table
e) *kitaku* —a powerful, massive table, appropriate for a heavy suiseki

FIG. 220 Wooden stands to display complementary plants, bonsai, and suiseki
a) *jiban*—a wooden board about ½ inch thick, from a stump of black walnut
b) *jiban*—a wooden board about 1¼ inches thick, used for heavier suiseki
c) *shizen-taku*—a wooden board with the typical rootlike carvings
d) Slats assembled lengthwise. Slat ends are kept irregular to give the impression they were broken.

maki-dai	a very low table with rolled ends (see Fig. 218)
shizen-taku like	a table with natural legs; has the shape of a tree stump; *shizen* means natural; also, carved tables called *ne-joku* look very much the natural ones (see Fig. 221)
dana	stands of different shapes, often with asymmetrical shelves of various sizes (see Fig. 222)
kazari-dana	stands for large suiseki; *shohin-dana* are smaller stands (see Fig. 223)
shizen-ban	a board from a stump of walnut or hickory, 2–3 inches high, carefully treated with varnish or polish (see Figs. 136a, b); generally used for heavy and powerful suiseki
jiban very	also a stand from a stump of walnut or hickory, but only ¾ inch high (see Figs. 220a, b); used for smaller, lighter suiseki and for complementary plants (see Fig. 224); also some very flat stands (some only millimeters high) made of different woods, with irregular shape but with edges carefully finished; also stands in which broken branch holes are part of the design; all these stands are carefully made and surface completely finished
funa-ita	boards from old boats; often only brushed and waxed; used for displaying a suiseki, board shows the stone's age and nobility

FIG. 223 *Kazari-dana* or *shohin-dana* are always used for arrangements of different art objects. In this picture, a *mame-bonsai* (mini bonsai), a suiseki, and a complementary plant are displayed together.

FIG. 222 This shelf (*dana*) was made on the island of Bali. It is very stable, and its proportions (29½ inches long) are ideal for displaying suiseki.

If tree stumps are available, you can make stands (*shizen-ban*) out of them. Clean the stump first, removing any remaining soil. Then saw stump boards of different thicknesses (1–2 inches thick) and drill ⅛-inch holes in the middle of each board.

These holes often prevent the boards from cracking. Next, carefully polish the boards with sandpaper (see "Practical Making of a Wooden Base") and treat the surface with wax or other products. In Asia, such wooden boards are lacquered several times with a colorless product

FIG. 221 This two-level *shizen-taku* is from China. On the bottom level is a *biseki* of a Buddhist priest. The top level shows a bottle-painting technique used in central China. On the left is a character from a Chinese fable. (Collection of W. Benz, 5½ inches high.)

133

(sometimes up to 10 times). As mentioned earlier, a suiseki in a *suiban* should be displayed low enough that the observer can look inside the tray and see into the "landscape." This is also important for suiseki with "mountain lakes." On the other hand, suiseki with *daiza* should be displayed nearly at eye level, so that it is possible to see their "best side" without effort. However, because of spatial constraints, this is not always the case. I have visited a number of suiseki exhibitions and galleries in Asia in which the suiseki with *daiza* were displayed in a position that was too low. For the viewer, the best angle of vision for observing suiseki ranges from 0–20 degrees (see Fig. 213).

This means that at a distance of about 40 inches from the suiseki, the eyes should be 9¾–11¾ inches above the center of the displayed object.

A bonsai table with high legs is often not sufficient to put the suiseki at eye level, but it is better in this position than closer to the floor. Suiseki placed on high tables for display sometimes seem unnatural and lacking in harmony. Thus, to preserve the harmony between the suiseki and the table, the observer is forced to sit or to bend down if he wants to be in the right position.

FIG. 224 On a *jiban*, a complementary plant (accent plant) on the left, a suiseki a little bit off center, and a mini bonsai on a *shizen-taku* on the right.

Complementary Plants (Accent Plants), Different Plant Species

Complementary plants (see Fig. 225) are important exhibition subjects for optimal displays of bonsai, penjing, or suiseki. In China and Japan, a complementary plant is any plant displayed with suiseki, bonsai, or penjing which contributes to the harmony of the arrangement. The plant should match the color of the main object (suiseki or bonsai). It is chosen as an accent to the suggested seasonal theme. In addition to matching colors, the shape and size of complementary plants must also be considered in connection with the main object.

Centuries ago, very simple plants were generally used for display, such as grass, *Ophiopogon japonicus*, or other wild plants. Today, many small perennials and grasses are appropriate as complementary plants (see Figs. 227, 228). Because of the great diversity, some grasses and flowering plants must be mentioned by their Latin names.

FIG. 225 View of a bonsai garden in Omiya, specializing in *mame* bonsai and complementary plants. The owner, a student of Mr. Hideo Kato, is an excellent ceramist.

FIG. 226 In this picture of complementary plants and in the preceding picture, we can see the great diversity of shapes and colors of plant containers. The materials range from ceramic to glass paste.

Appropriate Complementary Plants

Grasses and ferns:

Bouteloua gracilis

Briza maxima

Carex humilis

Carex montana

Davallia mariesli

Eleocharis congesta

Equisetum hiemale

Festuca scoparia

Hakonechloa macra Aureola

Imperata cylindrica (see Fig. 229)

Juncus effusus

Koeleria glauca

Luzula pilosa

Miscanthus sinensis

Molinia caerulea

Osmunda cinnamonea

Pennisetum alopecurtoides

Phalris arundinacea

Rume acetosella

Spiranthes sinensis

FIG. 227 Complementary plant—*Sempervivum arachnoideum* with dwarf pink.

FIG. 228 A variety of *Armeria maritima* in a *tokoname* container as a complementary plant for a suiseki.

FIG. 229 Grasses are very good complementary plants. This grass, *Imperata cylindrica*, already has its midsummer red tips.

FIG. 230 Many flowering plants can be used as complementary plants, such as *Prunella vulgaris* in this example.

136

Flowering plants:

Acantholimon glumaceum
Aeginetia indica
Ajuga reptans
Allium thunbergii
Androsace carnea
Antennaria dioica 'Rubra'
Aquilegia flabellata
Armeria maritima
Artemisia schmidtiana
Campanula punctata
Cyclamen purpurascens
Dianthus gratianopolitanus
Dianthus plumarius
Dianthus superbus
Draba sibirica
Dryas octopetala
Epilobium
Epimedium diphyllum
Epimedium grandiflorum
Equisetum
Erinus alpinus
Erythronium dens-canis
Habenaria
Houttuynia cordata
Hylotelephium pluricaule 'Rose Carpet'
Iris gracilipes
Iris sanguinea

Lewisia cotyledon
Lychnis alpina
Mukdenia rossii
Oenothera rosea
Polygonum japonicum
Potentilla aurea
Pritzelago alpina
Prunella vulgaris
Ranunculus
Rosularia
Rubus buergeri
Sanguisorba offinsinalis
Saxifraga × *rendsii*
Saxifraga paniculata
Saxifraga stolonifera
Scutellaria
Sedum album
Sedum spathulifolium
Semperivivum arachnoideum
Silene uniflora
Sisyrinchum angustifolium
Taraxacum
Thalictrum
Thymus vulgaris
Tricyrtis hirta
Veronica
Viola japonica
Viola odorata

Annual grasses

Annual grasses used as complementary plants are truly interesting decorations. Some of them have long flowering periods. Moreover, they thrive in poor soils. Always sow several seeds of a grass species together (see Figs. 231a and 231b). This way, the grasses establish compact root balls. You can easily plant them in bonsai containers.

Sow in the spring (between March and May) in wooden or plastic boxes in clumps.

You can also sow annual grasses right in the container which will be used for display. The soil should be prepared compost or an equal mix of screened garden soil, peat, and sand.

Different sorts of grasses need frost before they sprout, and they must be sown in autumn.

You can buy seeds in garden shops or nursery gardens.

FIG. 231a If possible, use soft water on the seeds. Sow annual grasses directly into the display container. Generally, one seed produces only one blade of grass.

Annual Grasses Which Are Excellent Complementary Plants:

Name	Flowering period	Height in inches
Agrostis nebulosa	July–October	15¾
Avena sterilis	July–August	7¾
Briza maxima	May–August	15¾
Lagurus ovatus	May–August	15¾
Lamarckia aurea	June–July	11¾

Grass seasons

Like other plants, many grasses, for example fresh green sprouts, seasonal stalk colors, flowers, or fruits, have a specific culminating point in the year. In winter, persistent grasses do best. There are spring grasses, summer grasses, autumn grasses, and winter grasses. Knowing this, we are able to make different displays according to each season. Some grasses are mentioned in the following table.

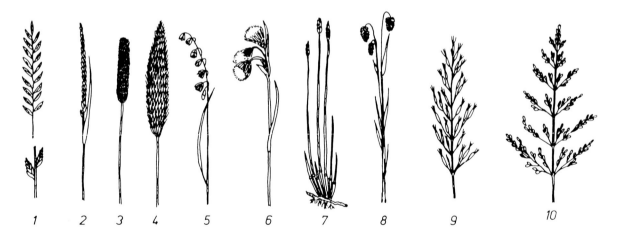

FIG. 231b Spikes of different grasses
(1) *Lolium multiflorum* (2) *Cynosurus cristatus* (3) *Alopecurus myosuroides* (4) *Alopecurus pratensis* (5) *Melica nutans* (6) *Eriophorum gracile* (7) *Juncus trivialis* (8) *Briza maxima* (9) *Avenochloa pubescens* (10) *Poa pratensis*

Spring Grasses

Name	Flowering period	Height in inches
Carex montana	end of March	7¾
Carex morrowii	end of March	11¾
Carex umbroso	from April on	15¾
Luzula pilosa	from April on	9¾
Sesleria albicans	from March on	7¾
Sesleria nitida	from April on	11¾

Summer Grasses

Name	Flowering period	Height in inches
Bouteloua gracilis	from July on	11¾
Luzula nivea	from June on	9¾
Melica ciliata	from May on	15¾
Poa glauca	from June on	4

Autumn Grasses

Name	Flowering period	Height in inches
Pennisetum orientale	September–October	15¾
Sesleria autumnalis	September–November	11¾

Winter Grasses

Name	Features	Height in inches
Carex plantaginea	persistent	4
Festuca scoparia	green in winter	4
Festuca vatesiaca	green in winter	6
Luzula maxima	persistent	9¾

Accessories

Figurines, Boats, Houses, Bridges, Pictures, Scrolls

The shapes of many suiseki suggest landscapes in a very precise way, often referring to specific seasons as well.

We can enhance this seasonal theme by placing a small figure, animal (see Fig. 232), house, bridge, or boat (see Fig. 233) in a *suiban* or close to the suiseki, bringing the display to life.

For example, adding a crab to a water pool stone (see Fig. 69) suggests moisture, even though the pool has no water in it.

However, use this technique sparingly or you'll end up with a kitschy display.

When choosing an object, examine the proportions between the suiseki and the figure, house, etc. carefully, especially when you're trying to create a perspective.

So, for example, when you want to place a boat in a lake, choose a small one for the back and a larger one for the front.

FIG. 233 Because fishermen generally leave very early in the morning, they define a precise moment of the day.

FIG. 234 This boy, playing a flute and riding a small buffalo, is only 1 inch high, and a true work of art. This type of bronze or ceramic figure is available in different sizes.

FIG. 232 When we see this water buffalo, we immediately think of nearby water or of wet land.

FIG. 235a Human figures—upper row: on the left, two musicians; on the right, men in different positions; lower row: cranes, a pavilion, and two sailing boats.

FIG. 235b Typical thatched-roof fishing huts; on the right, different types of boats.

141

FIG. 236 Simple *toko-noma* with a scroll in the background.

Every display requires great care, especially if we want to enhance its suggestive power.

You can find many different accessories. Most of them are made of clay. Sometimes, you can find complementary items in wood or bronze (see Fig. 234), but they are more expensive. In Japan and other countries in the Far East, a specific market has developed for these figures (see Fig. 235). They range in size from ½–7¾ inches and often have an artistic character.

Larger figures are rarely used to complement suiseki. In some displays, pictures or scrolls are used (see Fig. 236, Fig. 17). Often the subject of the scroll refers to one of the four seasons. In spring, a budding or flowering bonsai can be complemented with a scroll representing melting snow and a suiseki that has a small snow-covered peak and a large mountain stream. The presence of quartz veins indicating some remnants of snow makes a very harmonious display.

FIG. 237 Some scrolls have threads or fasteners to hold the pictures in place. This allows you to change the picture depending on the situation.

Instead of using a scroll, you can use a calligraphy of a spring poem. Suiseki lovers should acquire several pictures and scrolls so that they can arrange compositions in accordance with suggested themes.

In addition to ink drawings (*sumixe*) which are painted directly on the scroll paper, you can also find backgrounds provided with threads or other fasteners which allow you to change pictures (see Fig. 237). These permit you to fasten any picture or calligraphy you want to use, so that the scroll coincides with the season.

Colors, Color Wheel, Complementary Colors

White light contains all visible colors—the colors of the rainbow. We know that colors can strongly influence our moods. Depending on the color and the expressive decorations, we might be joyous, given to serious thinking, or even feel sad. A room can convey an impression of pleasant warmth or of icy cold. All green-yellow, yellow, and yellow-red colors are called warm tones; all blue-green, blue, and blue-red tones are cold tones (see Fig. 238). Black and white are not considered colors

143

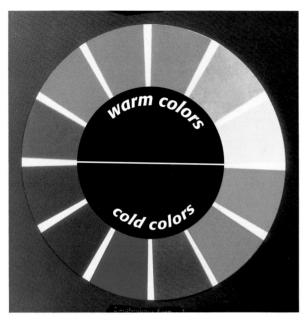

FIG. 238 A color wheel shows complementary colors and warm and cold colors.

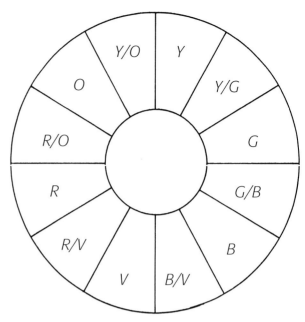

FIG. 239 Color wheel. Y = yellow, O = orange, R = red, V = violet, B = blue, and G = green.

on the color wheel. Dark and cold colors stimulate serious thinking and even sadness. Light and vivid color compositions produce an exciting effect; dark, flat colors are calming. Blue surfaces appear farther away than red ones. In a red sunset, mountains seem to be closer. By using corresponding colors, we can deceive the eyes about the real dimensions of a room.

An object reflects only the color of its surface. Red objects reflect red light, and green objects reflect green light. All other colors are absorbed.

This means that objects show their natural colors only when they are illuminated by white light. Artificial light is generally yellowish or reddish. When an object is illuminated by artificial light (rather than white light), there is a difference of color.

Rules for Combining Colors

Light tones match the shade tones of the same color. This is also true for colors next to each other on the color wheel and for opposite or complementary colors (see Fig. 239). Gray tones match all colors. Yellow-brown, brown, and red-brown tones nearly always match other colors, too. When you place a suiseki with its *daiza* on a wooden table, verify that the colors of the different woods do not contrast too much, and decide which color combination produces the best result. This is especially important when choosing an appropriate *suiban* or *daiza*. A blue-purple stone should be placed in a *suiban* filled with yellow-orange sand (see color wheel). According to the rules mentioned before, the glaze of the *suiban* could be blue, purple, or an intermediate color.

You can easily determine matching color combinations by using the color wheel. Complementary colors are red and green, blue and orange, yellow and purple, red purple and yellow-green, etc. These colors are opposite each other on the color wheel.

The Golden Section

Centuries ago, artists in the Far East discovered that some works convey a sense of balance and harmony, creating an illusion of truth. This truth results from an impression of harmony and three-dimensional space. European artists of the Middle Ages also learned to create this impression by using a mathematical rule in their picture compositions. When they were looking for rules, they discovered the precise proportions which build a special relationship. This is referred to as the golden section. These proportions can be defined in two ways:

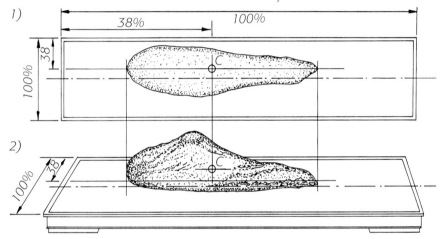

FIG. 240 Positioning a suiseki in a suiban according to the golden section.

■■ By using a mathematical series, such as the Fibonacci series, named after the Italian who first described it, we add the sum of the two preceding numbers:

$$1 + 1 = 2$$
$$1 + 2 = 3$$
$$2 + 3 = 5$$
$$3 + 5 = 8$$
$$5 + 8 = 13$$
$$8 + 13 = 21$$
$$13 + 21 = 34$$
$$21 + 34 = 55$$
$$34 + 55 = 89$$

If we take the last line for example, we can see that the number 34 represents about 38 percent of the number 89. This means that to create the golden section, we need to separate the two parts into 38 percent and 62 percent of the whole.

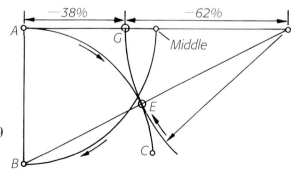

FIG. 241 A geometrical construction defining the golden section.

▌▌▌ We arrive at the same result with a geometrical construction (see Fig. 241). For this purpose, we first separate segment AD in the middle and use a compass to draw an arc from the middle of AD to point B, using point A as a base.

Then using point B as a base, we draw an arc from point A to C. A straight line from B to D cuts the second arc at E. If we take segment DE and use point D as a base, we obtain point G. Point G separates segment AD into two parts, according to the golden section (see Fig. 241).

In Europe, these principles of proportions were first used in architecture. Later, artists used them in painting and sculpture.

The golden section was first described by Vitruv in the treatise *De Architectura* to find the proportions of columns, rooms, and buildings.

"The ratio between two unequal parts of a given whole is equal to the ratio between the larger part and this whole."

The golden section was also used to define the ideal proportions of a rectangle. If the width corresponds to ⅝ of its length, the ratio between them is 0.618:1. During the Renaissance, the golden section was called the "divine proportion." In 1509, Leonardo di Vinci wrote a book with this title, and Albrecht Durer (1471–1528) wrote two treatises on the use of proportions: *Four Books on Human Proportion* (1557) and *Treatise on Measurement*. This significant principle defines ideal natural proportions, and it can be used in all artistic domains, including the arts of bonsai and suiseki (see Figs. 209, 215).

Correct Viewing, Visual Perception

Field of vision, appropriate distance of observation

A normal person's field of vision covers the space included in a cone with an angle of about 60 degrees. This is the viewing direction. The surface in the front is called the field of vision. When a subject is larger than the field of vision and we cannot change our position, we have to move our eyes, observe parts of the subject one after the other, memorize them, and mentally put them together again to get the whole picture. This is difficult. It requires effort to clearly see parts at the edge of the field of vision without modifying the direction of the look. But with a smaller field of view, with an angle of about only 40 degrees, we can easily perceive all the parts at the edge of this limited field of vision. Thus, from a distance of 40 inches, we can easily perceive objects that are 28¼ inches wide (see Fig. 242).

Therefore a *suiban* that is 40 inches wide can only be observed properly and comfortably from a distance of at least 55 inches. The length of time required for observation must be long enough, if we want to evoke the suggestive power of a suiseki.

When objects are too near, we tend to strain our eyes. Therefore, it is better to choose longer distances rather than shorter ones. Moreover, with longer distances, three-dimensional objects do not appear distorted. With *suiban* arrangements and complements (figures, bonsai, etc.), we achieve a better perspective with longer distances.

The appropriate distance is about two to four times the largest picture size or its diagonal dimension. For example, for a *suiban* with a suiseki that is 3 feet wide (see Fig. 242), the appropriate distance ranges from 6 to 12 feet.

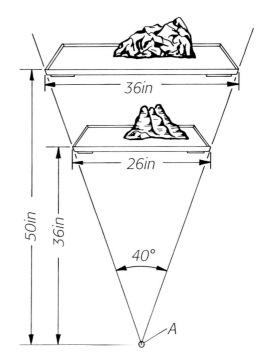

FIG. 242 Illustration of the field of vision for the correct distance of observation.

Structured (geometric) viewing

According to its shape and pattern, you can mentally cut a suiseki into geometric parts (see Fig. 243a).

You can consider all the basic geometric forms, such as circles, rectangles, squares, triangles, trapezoids, etc. After having determined the geometric parts of the subject according to its outer shape and lines, you can superimpose the geometric figures in your mind (see Fig. 243b). This picture reveals the dynamics concealed in the suiseki (see Figs. 244, 245a, 245b).

Moreover, structured viewing helps to determine the movement lines in objects which are otherwise difficult to evaluate.

FIG. 243a Example of structured (geometric) viewing. The starting point is this suiseki.

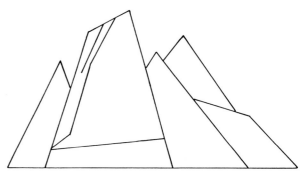

FIG. 243b The suiseki represented in Fig. 243a is cut out in geometric patterns (triangles and trapezoids). By superimposing geometric patterns, we achieve a dynamic view of the suiseki.

147

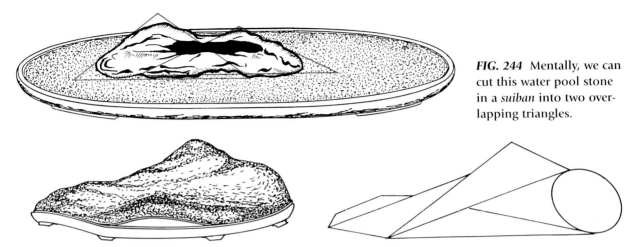

FIG. 244 Mentally, we can cut this water pool stone in a *suiban* into two overlapping triangles.

FIG. 245a A slope stone. Typically, we need a thorough observation before we can cut stones with such smooth outlines into geometric shapes.

FIG. 245b Here, we have tried to represent geometrically the slope stone seen in Fig. 245a.

Movement lines, direction of movement

The shape of each stone creates a given direction of movement. For example, a mountain stone has a peak and slopes down to a plateau or even directly to the base. When the peak is placed on the left side, as shown in Fig. 247, the movement is oriented towards the right side. We must place this mountain in a tray so that it has enough empty space in the direction of movement. To create the best position, we would place the visual central point of the stone according to the golden section of the tray.

Lines indicate the movement of a suiseki (see Fig. 246). This point is especially important when displaying stones in a tray or in a *tokonoma*, for example. By positioning the suiseki asymmetrically, the largest empty space will be on the side of the tray or *tokonoma* showing the direction of movement (see Fig. 246). In a *suiban*, this suggests a vast plain or a vast landscape; with water, it is the vast sea. The same is true for a bonsai or ikebana in a *tokonoma*.

FIG. 246 While observing this picture, we have the impression that, starting with the largest peak, the smaller ones are moving to the right. The arrow indicates the direction of the movement.

FIG. 247 The asymmetry of this mountain range clearly indicates movement towards the right side.

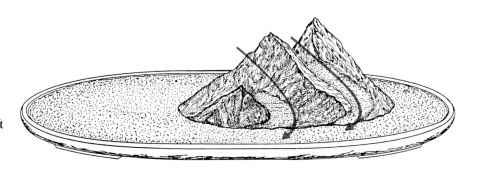

FIG. 248 Both lines of movement curve to the left side because of the structure of the stone.

The direction of movement always indicates the dynamics of a stone (see Fig. 247), but this does not mean that the direction is always a straight line. Depending on the shape of the stone or bonsai, the line may change direction (see Fig. 248) or even undulate. We must identify the movement before placing a stone in a tray or *tokonoma*.

Some stones have no clear direction, such as a symmetrical waterfall stone. The "water" in the stone would suggest a vertical descending movement. We might place this type of stone slightly back from the middle of the tray.

However, this would create a very static display. If we place the stone only ¼–½ inch to one side, we avoid a stiff impression. The overall picture is harmonious and no longer conveys "mathematical severity."

By using an asymmetrical position, we produce harmony when we place the visual central point of the subject (suiseki or bonsai) in the available space (tray or *tokonoma*) according to the golden section.

Viewing is an effort for the body and the mind. Depending on the object, the body tires more or less quickly, and the mind is bored or aroused.

When viewing produces a feeling of well-being, the resulting harmony satisfies our sense of beauty in relation to shapes, dimensions, and colors.

When something that is stirring our attention is at the limit of our field of vision, our eyes move from one point to another to see these details. Our eyes are guided from one point to the next, quickly if the object is familiar, slowly if it is something surprising and new.

FIG. 249 Open the book, place it about 10 inches in front of you, and try to see both subjects at the same time. You will probably find it difficult.

Fig. 250 Again, open the book, place it about 10 inches in front of you, and try to see all three subjects at the same time. Your eyes will probably move to the suiseki in the center.

Two attractive objects should not be too close to each other, or the eyes will become restless. The two objects displayed in Fig. 249 are so close that, at normal reading distance (about 10 inches), they are both in the observer's field of vision. However, the eyes cannot see them both at the same time. The eyes move restlessly from one to the other. If we add a third object between them, the eyes are attracted to the object in the center (see Fig. 250). In this example, a suiseki is the center of attention, and the two complementary objects play only supporting roles.

This whole subject follows the rules of composition (see "The Golden Section") about the separation of surfaces and the arrangement of several objects in a display. During suiseki and bonsai exhibitions, we frequently observe some kind of uniformity and repetition.

For example, we can correct the lack of diversity in simple shapes (see Fig. 251a) by adding other shapes as a contrast (see Fig. 251b).

The rectangles and balls symbolize objects on display, such as bonsai, suiseki, ikebana, and others.

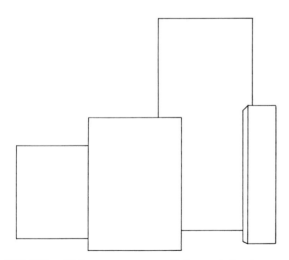

FIG. 251a   This arrangement of shapes is boring.

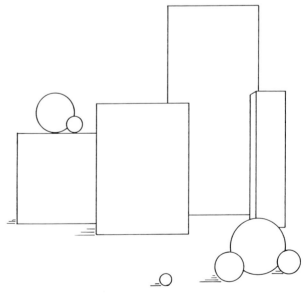

FIG. 251b   Adding balls brings the picture to life.

150

Photographing Suiseki, Bonsai, and Penjing

Most suiseki lovers own small cameras. I took all the color photographs in this book with a small camera. For most of the photographs, I only had a minute or so to take the shot. These pictures are all quite natural. The other ones have a studio character. Photographs made by a hobbyist are documents which record the changes in a suiseki or bonsai over several years. Such pictures must focus on the essential elements which require some sort of follow-up. The best photographs are taken under diffused daylight, with no direct sunlight.

Sunset is also a good time to take such pictures. Use ISO 50 and ISO 100.

Don't use a flash unless you know how to use it properly. If you use a front flash with an off-white background, your pictures will have shadows. This is very disturbing.

You'll have good results with a large depth of field using an f-stop between 16 and 32. Long exposure times are sometimes necessary, and this requires the use of a tripod and remote shutter release, but it also produces very good pictures. Don't use your auto-focus for these pictures.

Focus manually using the following method:

1. Set your f-stop.

2. Set the corresponding exposure time.

3. Place a ⅜-inch square piece of cardboard directly in front of the object you want to photograph.

4. Focus and remove the cardboard.

5. Shoot the picture.

In the photography group that I managed in Heidelberg, we used lamps for diffused light and spots for special effects, as well as several electronically synchronized flashes. We documented all the values on a form specifically designed for this purpose (see Fig. 252). In this way, we could reproduce exactly the conditions of any photograph.

Professional photographs

Use a table with a background (cloth, paper in different colors, flat-colored sheet, etc.), a top reflector (wooden panel covered with white paper, matte synthetic foil with gradual brightening of color, or piece of rigid plastic), two (or more) electronically synchronized flashes, two (or more) lamps, small cameras of different manufacturers, and a tripod. The arrangement of flashes and lamps is represented schematically in Fig. 252. This produces very good pictures, but it is not always necessary.

151

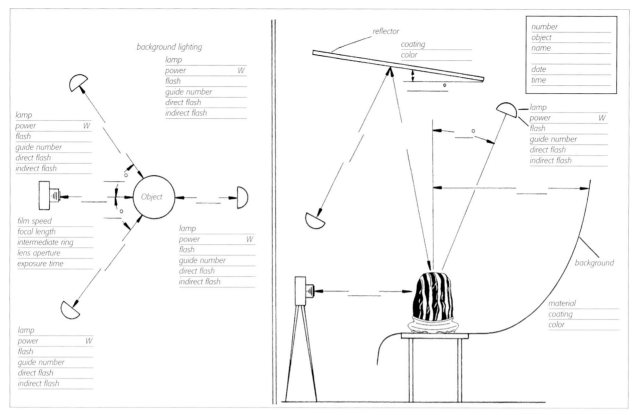

FIG. 252 Form used to write down all important values for photographs.

Simplified photograph techniques that produce good results

You can produce excellent results without a flash if you use a table with a background.

The choice of the color for the background (synthetic foil with gradual brightening of the color) is very important because the color has a major influence on the resulting contrast. Test different colors and write down the results. This way, you can plan ahead when you want to take photographs. You'll have good results with beige, blue gray, and dark gray (all colors blended with white).

Using a white piece of rigid plastic as a reflector may create enough light.

Taking photographs with small apertures

Taking photographs with a small aperture generally creates a smaller depth of field. But you can use this to your advantage. With the help of a telephoto lens with a focal length of 28–34 inches, the front of the object can be in focus. The background is out of focus with smaller apertures. However, this technique represents a compromise between depth of field and a fuzzy background.

Display and Exhibition of Suiseki, Bonsai or Penjing, and Ikebana

Years ago, when the arts of bonsai and suiseki were first introduced in the West, people used the literal translation of bonsai as "a tree in a container" and the literal translation of suiseki as "water stone." When asked about bonsai, most people still think of small miniature trees in ceramic containers. When asked about suiseki, some people aren't even sure if they can use the word in polite company. Obviously, the general public's knowledge about this art form is still rather limited. All of the answers contain a small spark of truth, but clearly bonsai and suiseki mean much more than what we get from a literal translation. The art of bonsai and the

FIG. 254 A beautiful mesa mountain from Indonesia. (Collection of G. Benz, 15¾ inches long.)

art of suiseki are difficult to understand because they are connected to other arts, philosophies, and cultures.

"Mr. X is the biggest penjing maker in northern China." "Today, Mr. Y is the best bonsai maker in the world." "This bonsai or this suiseki, situated in garden A, is the best one of its kind." "This is the best bonsai or the best suiseki of the exhibition." All of these remarks come from people who have not yet realized the true spiritual content of bonsai and suiseki.

Art is not absolute, such as, for instance,

"the best," "the most beautiful," and so on. The mood of the moment and the surrounding atmosphere play a prominent part. The encounter with a work of art (suiseki, bonsai, etc.) conveys a feeling of joy which is difficult to describe. For the observer, the feelings create a pattern that stays anchored for a long time. The memory of this encounter returns years later. This is all a subjective feeling. The same encounter experienced by different people at the same time produces different results.

From a coarse tree, an experienced bonsai maker can create an attractive object. It is obvious that the creation requires a minimal amount of technical skill. However, only after another ten or more years will we see if the maker has created a masterpiece. This is the same for a balanced and harmonious suiseki display.

We should learn the difference between art and technical knowledge, and we should avoid using literal translations. A bonsai is much more than a tree in a container, and a suiseki is something other than a stone in water. Behind the notions of bonsai and suiseki is a way of looking at things that has existed for centuries.

When observing a work of art, such as a suiseki, we "suffer martyrdom," to classify our own impressions correctly. Western-ers must make an effort to acquire sufficient knowledge of the different Eastern philosophies and mythologies in order to understand the arts of suiseki and bonsai. During my many trips to the Far East, I realized that my understanding of these art forms and their connections to other art forms was slowly growing.

Even natives sometimes have difficulty understanding the arts of the Far East, as we in the West may experience problems understanding our own arts (see Fig. 255). But this cannot prevent us from enjoying inner quiet with the arts of bonsai, ikebana, and suiseki. A good display of any of these is a way to create a harmonious connection with nature.

Many lovers of bonsai and suiseki don't give enough consideration to their display.

FIG. 255 Is it a modern sculpture or a suiseki?

FIG. 256 Display alcove or *tokonoma* in the bonsai museum of the Crespi family near Milan.

The idea is to enhance the suggestive power of a suiseki. Even after years have passed, an observer will recall such "living pictures." The impression determines how long a person can intensively recall a bonsai, ikebana, or suiseki display. Obviously, impressions can be either positive or negative. In the case of a display, we're much more interested in the positive side.

The deeper the positive impression, the more successful the arrangement of suiseki with other art objects will be.

For display, we have to follow some basic rules (see also "Correct Viewing, Visual Perception"), which we will present in the following pages. In general, we want to have few objects in the display alcove (see Figs. 256, 17). This alcove should

have a neutral background which matches the color of the displayed objects. In this way, the observer concentrates his attention on the suiseki. The less the background distracts from the displayed object, the more the suiseki can capture the attention of the observer. The background for a suiseki display should be plain. It has to enhance the displayed object and to put it clearly in the field of vision. A wide open space will lose the image because of distraction.

A supplementary light shows the displayed object to full advantage, especially when the contours of the suiseki need to be emphasized.

In most cases, the appropriate colors for a background are light gray, matte white, or beige. We don't want to see its surface texture distinctly.

A suiseki display should not be simply a collection of plants and objects in the alcove. More than three objects would be too much. Fewer objects are more impressive than many. When displaying two or three objects, we must consider the proportions (see Figs. 257a, 257b) and fit the objects together in such a way that we create as much harmony as possible.

All the elements added to the main object, such as stands, tables, complementary plants, and so on, must be chosen carefully and must match the color of the main object. They should never usurp the role of the main object. Rather, they should enhance the suggestive power of the primary object.

There are several ways of displaying suiseki, bonsai, and ikebana:

▌▌▌ *tokonoma*
A special alcove (see Figs. 256, 17) built in traditional Japanese homes for *kazari* (display of bonsai, ikebana, suiseki, and complementary plants).
▌▌▌ *yoma-kazari*
A Western-style room used for displaying suiseki or bonsai.
▌▌▌ *seki-kazari*
A display of objects in special booths used for exhibitions.
▌▌▌ *niwa-kazari*
A display of bonsai or suiseki in a garden or on a patio.

FIG. 257a With two objects or more in a reduced space, size proportions must be respected. Here, the crab is too large for the stone.

FIG. 257b Here, the size of the crab is right. Moreover, there is a contrast of color between the two objects, and this emphasizes the crab.

In the Far East, many houses have a display area where valuable objects, such as bonsai, penjing, suiseki, ikebana compositions, sculptures, pictures, and calligraphy can be exhibited. They are changed now and then for the pleasure of both the owner and the guests.

For the best possible result, seventy-five to eighty percent of the space in the alcove must remain empty. Never place the primary subject, such as a suiseki or bonsai, dead center. Instead, place it to the side, thus avoiding a rigid display and creating inner movement and suggestive power. The choice of left or right side depends on the light conditions, the shape of the suiseki (each one has a best side), and the complementary object. Present the best side to the front. The shape indicates the movement and determines the position of the suiseki (see "Movement Lines, Direction of Movement").

Try to find the most harmonious composition for each display.

Sometimes it is difficult and time-consuming to determine the best arrangement.

We Distinguish between Two Major Groups of Suiseki:

▌▌▌ **Outdoor suiseki**
▌▌▌ **Indoor suiseki**

Outdoor suiseki

Suiseki displayed in gardens and parks must be large enough to be seen among other objects such as trees, bushes, and rocks. Choose a place where the background conveys a sense of calm (see Figs. 5, 6) and brings the suiseki to the forefront. The choice of an appropriate position in relation to nearby plants is especially important for a harmonious picture in every season. Other objects should not be competing or distracting. The quality of the suiseki can be emphasized by choosing an appropriate base.

In ancient China, artisans created expensive and elaborate bases for this purpose (see Figs. 258, 259). Color and material play an essential part in a a successful display because they must harmonize with the surroundings.

FIG. 258 Chinese people have created artistic and elaborate bases for their outdoor suiseki. This is an example from the Emperor Garden in the Forbidden City in Beijing.

FIG. 259 This outdoor suiseki, a leopard-skin stone, sits on the terrace of a lake at the Summer Palace in Beijing. Note the reliefs on the base and socle.

Indoor suiseki

We can display suiseki many different ways in a house. For example, we can simply place the suiseki on a nice wooden board (see Fig. 260), a piece of cloth, a bamboo mat, or a beautiful table. The wooden board defines the space for observation. Our eyes automatically move to the surface defined by the board, piece of cloth, or bamboo mat, provided there is some color contrast between the stand and the surroundings. Choose the dimensions of the stand according to the size of the stone. For massive, powerful stones with round or cubic shapes, the wooden board should be three to five times longer. For high, slender stones, the diameter of the wooden board should be approximately equal to the height of the stone or a little smaller.

FIG. 260 Wooden boards and mats are frequently used to define space for the observer. This suiseki is placed on a board made of black walnut.

Rules for Displaying Suiseki in Containers, on Daiza, and on Tables

Suiseki in containers (*suiban, doban*)

The principal subject of the display is the suiseki. The container is an important complement. If chosen properly, it contributes quite a bit to the quality of the display. The following table lists some suggestions.

Suiseki type	Container
delicate, flat suiseki with slender shape	shallow tray with narrow sides; height ⅛ inch (see Fig. 210)
massive, powerful suiseki	heavy tray with thick sides; not too shallow; overall height ¾–1½ inch
vertical suiseki	simple shape; straight side profile
rugged and massive suiseki	large, heavy container with high sides; overall height 1–2 inches
old-looking suiseki with beautiful patina	bronze *suiban* (*doban, thung-suiban*) with a patina corresponding to that of the suiseki (see color wheel, Fig. 238)
colored suiseki	container with colors chosen from the color wheel; should not compete with the color of the suiseki

Based on the golden section

▌▌▌ The suiseki may be set in the container (*suiban, doban*) without water or sand when the bottom of the *suiban* or *doban* has a matching glaze.

▌▌▌ The container may be filled with fresh water when the features of the stone make it possible.

▌▌▌ The container may be filled with washed sand up to ⅛ inch below the lip.

▌▌▌ In addition to sand, the container may be filled with water.

▌▌▌ The container may be only partially filled with sand, when, for example, the color of the bottom suggests the water of a sea or lagoon.

▌▌▌ The container may be filled with sand and partially covered with low moss of some color.

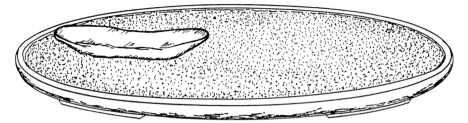

FIG. 261 The boat stone is placed on the left side. Because it "moves" to the right, it requires a larger empty space on the right side.

Bonsai containers are generally inappropriate for suiseki because they are too high. An adequate height for a standard suiseki is ¼–⅜ inch. Ikebana vases are also generally too high in addition to being too brightly colored. Unglazed ceramic containers (*suiban*) of gray, red brown, or dark brown are appropriate. Choose glazed ceramic containers (*suiban*) carefully, matching the color of the stone. We recommend dark blue, dark green, or dark gray. In a display, the stone becomes closely associated with the container (*suiban*). In addition to the color of the *suiban*, its size plays an essential part.

Choose a shallow container that is large enough for the proportions of the stone. An island stone or a boat stone only produces the desired effect when it has a large area of "water" around the stone. As a rule, choose a container two or three times the length of the stone. The shape tells us the direction a boat stone "moves" (see Fig. 261). Its position in the container is right when it is slightly behind the line running through the middle of the *suiban*, the bow of the boat facing a large area of "water." The captain of the boat would like to enjoy this journey as long as possible.

Placement of the Stone in the *Suiban/Doban*

Because of its shape, a suiseki has precise line structures which convey an image, starting at a mountain peak, for example (see Figs. 209, 247), and developing their own dynamics from top to bottom. We speak of the direction of Movement (see "Movement Lines, Direction of Movement"). This helps us to set a stone in a container in accordance with its own dynamics. We set the stone off-center so that the running lines have the largest free space. We create an ideal picture when we place the visual central point of the stone in accordance with the golden section of the container (see Fig. 262).

Some stones have no precise direction of movement or have a vertical direction, such as waterfall stones, for example. Generally, we set the visual central point of these stones in the *suiban* according to the golden section (see Figs. 263a, 263b, 263c).

If a container is a little too small for a stone, move the stone slightly behind the middle (according to the direction of movement and the golden section).

The golden section used to place a stone in a *suiban* applies to the length (see Fig. 262) and to the depth (see Figs. 264a, 264b, 264c, 240). We divide the width of the container into two parts, representing 38 percent and 62 percent of the whole.

The smallest part of the depth (38 percent) is at the back, and the largest is in front.

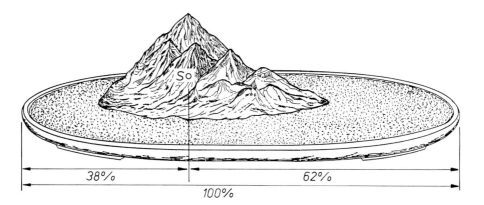

FIG. 262 The visual central point of this mountain is exactly above the golden section of the *suiban*.

38%   62%

100%

FIG. 263a This waterfall stone, found in the Cevennes (a dry waterfall), has a slight movement towards the left side. Therefore, it should have more space on the left side. (Collection of H. Brenner, Germany.)

FIG. 263b This time the waterfall stone is set nearly in the center. The arrangement is better, but still not right.

FIG. 263c Now, the visual central point is above the golden section of the *suiban*. This is the ideal placement for this suiseki.

161

a)

C

FIG. 264a The rule of the golden section may also be applied depthwise. This stone is too close to the front.

FIG. 264B The stone is set exactly on the imaginary horizontal line running through the middle of the suiban. This produces a very "severe" effect. In such a display, remember that the container seems very deep to the observer.

b)

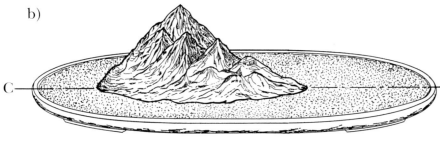

C

c)

C

FIG. 264c In this case, the visual central point is exactly at the intersection of the lines defined by the golden section of the container.

How Many Stones Is it Possible to Display in a *Suiban* or *Doban*?

Generally, we only set one stone in a *suiban* or *doban*. However, there are moments in everyday life when several people or animals meet together in very specific locations. This fact means that we can put several stones together in one container.

However, the arrangement must convey a clear "message."

Why Do We Use Sifted Sand or Fine Gravel?

Sand provides stability to an uneven stone, but it can also suggest different elements in relation to the surroundings of the stone. When a mountain stone is set in a *suiban* with sand, the sand represents the plain or the ground around the mountain. When an island stone is set in sand, the sand suggests surrounding water. With an object stone, sand could suggest a crowd, especially if the grains have a uniform size of about ⅛ inch. Use the evocative power of sand deliberately. Small crabs placed close to a water pool stone suggest wet sand, even if the pool is dry. From these examples, we can see that the color of the sand is important.

FIG. 265 The poet Li Ban is holding a dialogue with a *reiheki,* a coastal rock spirit found in Chinese mythology.

Using different colors of sand is not appropriate. If possible, all the grains of sand should have the same color. The best colors are shades of gray to white, beige to brown, or black (lava sand). Wash the sand carefully before using it, so that you remove most of the soil particles. Fill a deep container, a bucket for example, with sand up to a third of its depth. Then add water up to the rim. Stir the mixture vigorously. After a while, the grains of sand will fall to the bottom. Carefully pour out the dirty water. Repeat this process several times until the water remains nearly clear even after you stir it. Aquarium sand and birdcage sand are good choices.

Suiseki in containers are set below eye level. The observer must be able to look into the container. Placing the container on a nice table in the observer's field of view enhances the beauty of the suiseki.

Suiseki on Wood, Bronze, or Stone Bases (*Daiza*)

Wood, bronze, or stone bases (*daiza*) provide stability to a stone. These bases are sometimes very elaborate, and they enhance the display value of a suiseki. The criteria for choosing a *daiza* are described in "Making a Wooden Base."

We can display a suiseki on a *daiza* simply on a stand, a shelf (*kazari-dana*), or in a *tokonoma*. Setting a suiseki on a *daiza* on a low table (*kitaku* or *kitaru*) enhances its character (see Fig. 265).

Displaying Objects on Tables

A suiseki on a *daiza* is generally viewed horizontally; a suiseki in a shallow container is always displayed below eye level. The distance between the suiseki and the observer should be 1½–3 times the length of the tray or the height of the suiseki (see "Correct Viewing").

Set flat suiseki on tables of average height (about 6 inches), or on high ones (12–15¾ inches). Tall, slender suiseki are practically always presented on low tables or wooden boards. Massive, powerful suiseki are set on stable tables.

When we set a suiseki in a *suiban* on a table or board, the ratio of the height of the table to the height of the suiseki varies from 2:1–7:1. In other words, the table should be two to seven times higher than the suiseki.

Either in a container or on a *daiza*, never place the suiseki exactly in the center of the table (see Fig. 266).

When the movement of a suiseki is towards the right side, leave more empty space on the right. Set the suiseki off-center on the left side. The same rule applies for a stone in a container. Pay attention to the movement of the stone. Display a flat suiseki only on a low and long table, especially if it has an elongated shape (see Figs. 267, 268, 269).

For a suiseki with an asymmetrical shape, the visual central point and the container should be set off-center. The length of the table should be 1½–2 times the length of the container.

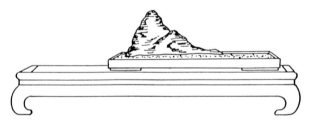

FIG. 266a When displaying a suiseki in a *suiban* on a table, don't place the container exactly in the center of the table. This stone shows movement towards the right side, so its position is wrong. The container is too far to the right.

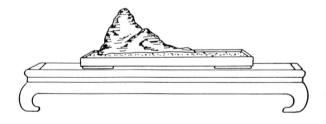

FIG. 266b In this case, the container is nearly in the center, a much better placement.

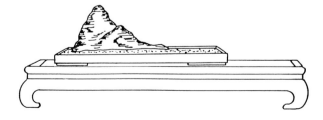

FIG. 266c In this picture, the container is too far to the left. This creates too much tension. The best placement would be a compromise between the one in Fig. 266b and this one.

FIG. 267 This table is too high and too short. It would have been better to set the suiseki in a container and the container on a larger table, according to the rules discussed in Fig. 266.

FIG. 268 A small mountain on a *maki-dai* (rolled stand) that is much too short.

FIG. 269 When we look at this picture, we see the table first. Only then do we discover the suiseki, which is much too long for this table.

Rules for Displaying Suiseki in Alcoves and Similar Places

First, we ask the following questions:

▮▮ Do we need a wooden base (*daiza*) to display the stone?

▮▮ Would it be better to place the stone in a tray filled with sand?

▮▮ Which shape would be best for the wooden base?

▮▮ Would a bonsai produce the desired effect as a complementary object, or would a plant (grass, fern, etc.) be better?

▮▮ Could a calligraphy or scroll painting add something to the arrangement?

▮▮ Which should be placed higher, the suiseki or the complementary object?

▮▮ What is the appropriate size for the table?

FIG. 270 In this painting, the artist used the three-distance divided perspective: the lower third is the closest, the middle third is intermediate, and the upper third is the farthest away.

Principle of the divided perspective

Chinese landscape painters of the Sung period (960–1279 A.D.) were not aware of central perspective. To give their pictures depth, they separated them into three parts and divided each artistically with a hazy veil or empty space (see Fig. 270).

The bottom third illustrated the closest area. All the objects were relatively large and very precise. The middle part of the surface showed the intermediate distance in the open (600–3,000 feet away from the painter). In this area, all the objects were correspondingly smaller and less precisely represented.

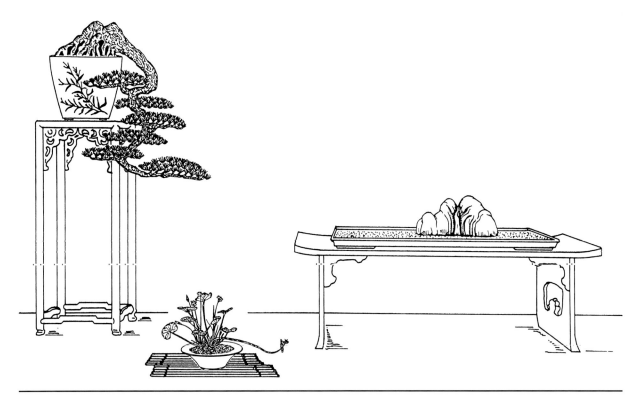

FIG. 271 Example of a display with three objects in a *tokonoma* (simplified representation). The bonsai cascade represents the far distance; the waterfall stone represents the intermediate distance; and the marsh marigold represents the closest area.

FIG. 272 The previous picture (see Fig. 271) can produce the illusion of a complete landscape. The distinctive shape of the bonsai represents a mountaintop, the needle clusters can be compared to small mountain forests, and the tortuous trunk could correspond to a mountain path. The water of the waterfall must flow downwards. Because marsh marigolds often grow in humid and wet places, a mountain stream could run along the plant.

The upper part of the surface was reserved for remote elements and clouds. In this area, the mountains and other objects were imprecise and often a little blurred.

The Chinese had specific words for each type of viewing

Looking into the distance was called *yüan-chin*. Looking from the base to the top—the high distance—was called *kao-yüan*. Looking above the mountain peaks in the foreground to a mountain range in the distance was called the deep "distance," or *shen-yüan*. Looking across a flat landscape to remote mountains—the level distance—was called *pin-yüan*. An empty surface suggested every possibility.

Indeed, although these paintings have no true perspective, they present great depth. We can use the principle of painting with three-distance perspective when we display three objects in a *tokonoma* (see Figs. 271, 272). For example, we could use a plant, a suiseki (or a bonsai), and a scroll in the background. In this case, the complementary plant sits in the front (the closest area of landscape painting), the suiseki or bonsai is placed behind (corresponding to the intermediate distance of landscape painting), and the scroll on the back wall represents the far distance. In this case, only scrolls or paintings of blurred objects are appropriate.

Suiseki Displays on Stands

The creation of stands with asymmetrical shelves (see Figs. 273, 274, 275) has a long tradition in Asia. In addition to artistic considerations, careful workmanship is highly valued. Most of the wood used for this purpose is very expensive, for example cherry, pear, rose, mahogany, rosewood, and teak. The stands are waterproofed. Then they are dyed, varnished, lacquered, or treated with wax (palm wax or beeswax).

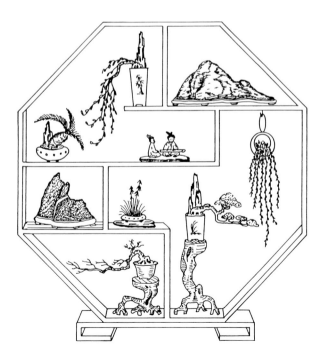

FIG. 273 This octagonal stand with asymmetrical shelves works well when the height is limited.

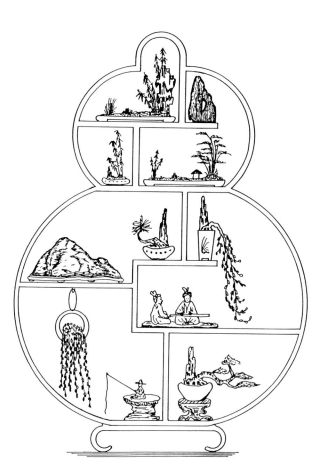

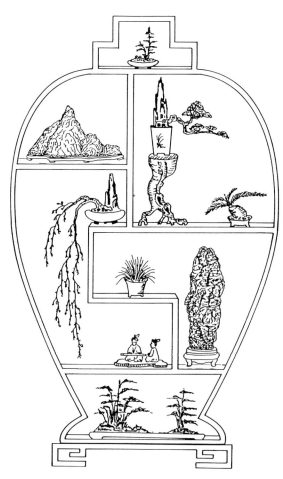

FIG. 274 The Chinese appreciate this stand in the shape of a calabash or gourd.

FIG. 275 A stand shaped like a vase is also a typical Chinese shape for display stands.

FIG. 277 This asymmetrical three-level stand is very elaborate. It is only 9⅞ inches high and is designed to display miniature suiseki.

FIG. 276 This stand for mini bonsai, suiseki, and other art objects is at the entrance to the Garden of Hidden Beauties in Singapore.

FIG. 278 The ornamental bamboo of this stand is typical of Chinese craft work, too. The stand is 21¼ inches high and could be used for displaying small works of art. Only the upper shelf has room to display larger objects.

Generally, the outer frames of such stands have geometrical outlines, such as square, hexagonal, or octagonal. However, sometimes they also have the shape of fans, vases, or calabashes. When the outer frame is symmetrical, the inner sections are always asymmetrical. For example, it is possible that an asymmetrical shelf stops suddenly, leaving an empty space.

The different shelves are filled with valuable objects, such as miniature bonsai, figures, teapots, complementary plants, miniature landscapes, and also with suiseki (see Fig. 276). Such stands are 8 inches to 6 feet high. The diversity of objects displayed offers a living picture. If enough objects are available, it is possible to create several variations in the display (see Figs. 277, 278).

170

Bonsai and Suiseki Displayed in a *Tokonoma*

▌▌▌ *shin* display

The *shin* display is a very formal, slender, vertical composition of art objects. We use bonsai, especially conifers such as pines or junipers, in the formal upright, slanting, cascade, or informal upright styles and present the bonsai with a scroll in the background. The bonsai is on one side at a distance from the back wall equal to about 40 percent of the depth of the alcove. The suiseki is on the other side in the foreground at a distance from the back wall that is equal to about 60 percent of the alcove depth. The scroll is a calligraphy, a painting, or a drawing. For the calligraphy or picture, the theme must emphasize the theme intended by the display.

Another combination, also classified as *shin* display, would be a scroll representing sunset waves breaking on rocks, and a suiseki such as an island stone in a *suiban* filled with sand and water and placed on a table about 12 inches high. This display would also have a complementary plant such as reed grass or sedge in a shallow, round, or slightly oval container, displayed on a coarse linen cloth or burlap, irregularly sprinkled with fine sand.

▌▌▌ *gyä* display

Compared to the *shin* display, the *gyä* display is less formal, often with a slight movement and more width than the severe *shin* form. Only deciduous trees such as maple, box, or elm are used in this type of display. We combine them with suiseki (animal and human shapes are also used) or with complementary plants. Many choices are possible, such as perennials or mountain grasses. The complementary plant sits on one side of the foreground, and the bonsai is in the background on the other side. The different objects must fit together.

▌▌▌ *sä* display

A *sä* display is very flexible, with strong movements and a lot of breadth. Here, too, we can use only two art objects. Suiseki are often combined with wild plants, colored grasses, dwarf rushes, dwarf bamboo, reeds, etc.

Complementary plants must fit with the suiseki as the main subject of the display.

For these three types of display, we must pay attention to ensure that the theme of the different objects is consistent.

Some examples:

▌▌▌ A scroll representing an eagle flying high above water, a suiseki, such as a flat island in a *suiban* filled with water, and a dwarf rush in a shallow container placed on a shallow wooden stand or on a reed matting.

▌▌▌ A scroll with a blurred landscape painting, a bonsai in the slanting style with its crown in the middle of the *tokonoma*, and a near-view landscape suiseki in a *suiban* filled with sand. This display would correspond to the principles of the three-distance perspective used in Sung ink painting.

FIG. 279 When we display three objects in a tokonoma, we must arrange the three so that the line joining the three visual central points describes an asymmetrical triangle.*

▓ A scroll with a calligraphy poem that evokes spring or a painting suggesting spring, an ikebana composition for the spring season, and a suiseki on a *daiza* with quartz or spar inlays representing a mountain with melting snow. Here, the suiseki should be in the foreground on a flat rootwood board (*jiban*).

▓ A calligraphy poem that evokes autumn, a landscape suiseki with autumn colors, and an ikebana composition or a complementary plant representing autumn.

▓ A scroll with an autumn theme, a bonsai with only a few leaves left, and some leaves on the moss ground. This bonsai would be on the floor of the *tokonoma*. A suiseki on a long table, 15¾ inches high, should suggest a mountainous landscape with peaks covered by the first snow.

When creating an arrangement, the most important principle is asymmetry (see Fig. 16). This asymmetry corresponds to the way many plants grow and, therefore, fits the requirement of our feeling of naturalness. The art of suiseki attaches much importance to the imagination of the observer and to inner movement. As a result of asymmetry, empty spaces are essential elements of the composition. The unevenness created by asymmetry forces the observer to experience new impressions, which is the inner meaning of the composition of such arrangements.

We would like to add one more rule. If we mentally draw lines between the visual central points of three objects placed in a display alcove, a *tokonoma*, the resulting triangle must be uneven (see Fig. 279). When we follow this rule, we create a dynamic experience, and we capture the attention of the observer.

* Can you find an error in this picture? Gerbera and pines don't form a natural group.

A suiseki display in the tea room

Essentially there are two types of display:

▌▌▌ *The surface of the scroll picture is oriented vertically.*

▌▌▌ *The surface of the scroll picture is oriented horizontally.*

If the surface of the scroll is oriented vertically, then we place a suiseki with its *daiza* before the scroll in such a position that the distance between its visual central point and the edge of the *tokonoma* equals 35–40 percent of the width of the whole *tokonoma* (see "The Golden Section"). This rule also applies to the depth of the alcove, so that we place the suiseki 40 percent of the distance from the back wall (see Fig. 280).

For a horizontally oriented picture, place the suiseki almost, but not exactly at, the center of the *tokonoma*.

In a tea ceremony for men, we would choose a suiseki with simple lines.

In a tea ceremony for women, we would prefer an elaborate suiseki, for instance a chrysanthemum stone. The distance from the back wall is also equal to about 40 percent of the size of the tatami matting, approximately 13½ inches.

FIG. 280 This picture, showing a typical display of a suiseki together with a scroll painting, is for a tea ceremony for women, because of the use of a chrysanthemum stone. The stone is very slightly to the right, while the scroll painting is oriented slightly to the left. This placement creates a weak tension.

173

A Two-Object Display in a *Tokonoma*

When two objects are placed in a presentation alcove, one of them must always dominate the other (see Figs. 281, 282, 283). Two objects with the same size appear to be too much. They seem very disturbing to the observer, whose eyes have to move back and forth between both objects, making it impossible to concentrate on either one of them. Suiseki masters, ikebana masters, and bonsai or penjing masters display their favorite objects in alcoves according to their feelings. After several hours, they look at the display again and make corrections, if necessary.

The observer must always be captured by the display. We speak of such a display as having a strong impressive power.

When we have given adequate attention to all the details mentioned here, we can consider the arrangement finished.

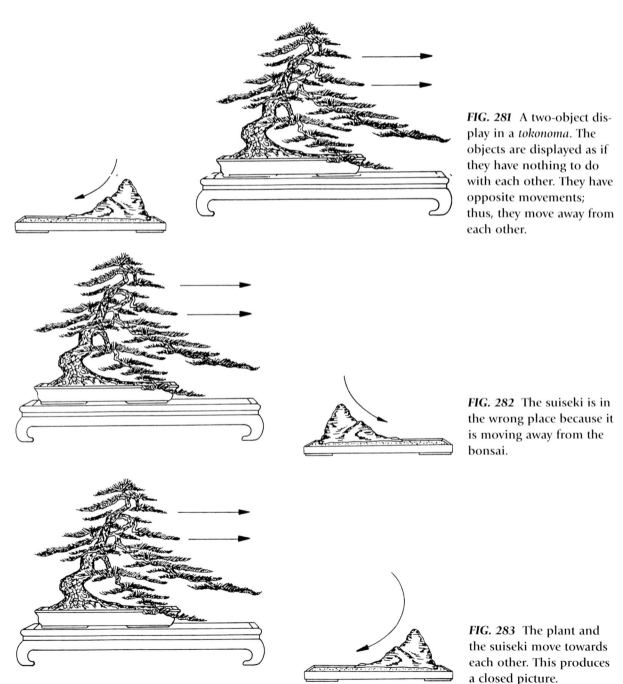

FIG. 281 A two-object display in a *tokonoma*. The objects are displayed as if they have nothing to do with each other. They have opposite movements; thus, they move away from each other.

FIG. 282 The suiseki is in the wrong place because it is moving away from the bonsai.

FIG. 283 The plant and the suiseki move towards each other. This produces a closed picture.

174

FIG. 284 A suiseki with a mask-shaped face in an eroded piece of palm root.

After carefully studying a display, ask yourself the following questions:
- Is there any way to enhance the artistic message of this arrangement?

- Is it a harmonious picture?

- Is the arrangement obtrusive?

- Can the observer understand the significance of the suiseki?

When all these questions are answered satisfactorily, only the quiet enjoyment of the display remains, because.....

How limited are
The spare times of life
at the end of autumn...

Buson (1716–1793)

Appendix
General notions

biseki

Beautiful stones. Strictly speaking, these are not suiseki, but they are often displayed with suiseki during exhibitions. *Biseki* are carved and polished to enhance their beauty. Many collectors prefer carved and polished stones to emphasize flower patterns or to add depth to the colors. Unlike suiseki, *biseki* do not need a suggestive shape.

bonkai

Landscape created with colored clay and artificial or dry miniature trees and grass.

bonkazan or *kazan*

Artificial mountain in a container (*suiban*).

bonsan

Natural mountain in a container.

bonseki

Dry landscape in a container. Black, lacquered trays are often used for this purpose. First the stones are placed. Then sifted white sand in nine different grain sizes is arranged in the tray with beautiful paintings.

chia shan

Chinese term for artificial mountains.

chu-taku

Medium to high stand for displaying bonsai and suiseki.

daiza, dai

Base generally made of wood, exactly adapted to each stone and used as a base. The *daiza* and the stone together form the suiseki.

doban

Watertight bronze containers (trays) used to display suiseki.

fumi-zuku-e

See *kitaru* (low table for an offering).

funa-ita

Board from the bottom of an old boat used to display bonsai and suiseki.

gia son

Vietnamese term for artificial mountains.

gyä display

Bonsai (usually a deciduous tree) displayed with a suiseki or complementary plant.

hakinowa

Miniature gardens in wood containers,

consisting of natural plants, stones, soil, and pieces of wood.

hira-dai

See *hira-taku.*

hira-taku

Wooden stand with very flat legs for displaying suiseki or complementary plants.

hsieh tzujing

Chinese term for miniature landscapes of different sorts, made with stones, sand, clay, water, and pieces of wood.

jiban

Thin, flat board, usually from a walnut or black walnut tree stump.

kazari-dana

Stand with two or more layers for displaying small bonsai or suiseki.

kitaku

Low table, especially made to display suiseki and bonsai.

kitaru

Low table, formerly used to hold an offering in temples (also in house temples); designed to display suiseki and bonsai.

kotaku

Tall stand used for cascade-style bonsai.

maki-dai

Very flat stand with rolled ends.

meiseki

Famous stones. This term is used for suiseki or biseki that are famous because of their extraordinary characteristics and beauty. Many of these stones have been passed down from generation to generation. They are generally kept in museums and in the palaces of kings and emperors.

miniature suiseki

Most are less than 3 inches high and less than 3–4 inches wide.

mon-yo-seki, mon-seki

Stones with extraordinary surface patterns, including minerals that show special structures and colors.

ne-joku

Table carved to look like roots.

niwa-ishi

Outdoor suiseki so large that they cannot be carried by one person.

niwa-kazari

Suiseki or bonsai displayed in the garden.

penwan

"Toy landscape" in a container, made of stones, sand, clay, water, pieces of wood with toy houses, bridges, roads, paths, lakes, boats, human beings, and animals.

rare stones

In these stones, the natural combination of several minerals with different colors produces attractive shapes or extraordinary pictures.

reiheki

"Steep cliff spirit." These Chinese stones are characterized by their sharp vertical lines, strongly eroded surfaces, complicated shapes, and tunnels.

saikei

Living miniature landscapes in a container (*suiban*); the Chinese term is *hsieh tzujing*.

seki-kazari

Suiseki displayed in special exhibition booths.

shan-shui penjing

Chinese miniature landscapes; compositions similar to *penwan*.

shin display

Bonsai (usually a conifer) displayed with a suiseki, a *koro* (incense burner), or a scroll (landscape painting or calligraphy).

shizen-ban

Thick natural wooden plate from a walnut stump, used for displaying bonsai and suiseki.

shizen-taku

Natural root stand; not to be confused with *ne-joku*.

shohin-dana

Stand used for mini bonsai or mini suiseki.

shoku

Table for displaying suiseki or bonsai.

sä display

Very flexible display in which a suiseki is presented with bamboo, rushes, grass, wildflowers, etc.

suiban

Watertight ceramic or lacquerware container.

suiseki

Literal translation is "water stone" (*sui* means "water," *seki* means "stone"). These are stones shaped by nature without any human manipulation. They suggest natural elements (people, animals, plants, mountains, etc.).

take-dai

Woven bamboo mat used for complementary plants, small bonsai or ikebana compositions, and occasionally suiseki.

taku

See *shoku* (table).

tatami mat

Rice straw mat 35 by 71 inches, mostly used to cover the floor in Japanese houses and in the *tokonoma*.

tokonoma

Special alcove in a traditional Japanese house where art objects such as bonsai, suiseki, ikebana, scrolls, and sculptures can be displayed. The guest of a Japanese family is generally seated in front of the *tokonoma* to enjoy the art objects arranged especially for him.

yuraiseki

Historical stones. These are suiseki or biseki owned by famous people or associated with notable historical events.

Aesthetic concepts

feng-liu (Chinese)

"Following the wind" or simply "elegant entertainment," the way of life of the Chinese scholars in the Middle Ages.

furyu (Japanese)

"Elegant entertainment" or "noble elegance," similar to the terms *shibui* and *shibusa*.

sabi (Japanese)

Concept which cannot be precisely described. It includes the notions: ancient, respectable, antique, mature, melancholic, lonely, subdued, seasoned, etc.

But *sabi* also implies a feeling for the transitory nature of things which are beautiful precisely because they are fleeting, for instance, the beauty of a suiseki or a bonsai which becomes older with time.

shibui (Japanese)

Concept that is difficult to describe accurately. It includes the notions: quiet, elegant, understated, reserved, reflective, polished, and refined.

wabi (Japanese)

Concept that cannot be precisely translated. It includes the notions: simple, lonely, melancholy, quiet, desolate, impoverished, and unpretentious. It is the subjective impression evoked by a picture representing a lonely fisherman's shack buffeted by a storm on a gray winter day. It presents an undefined mournful impression that is filled with the enjoyment of the magic contained in most simple things. *Wabi* is a feeling of the simplicity and naturalness of things. Together *sabi* and *wabi* convey an impression of quiet and serenity.

yoin (Japanese)

Means "echoing." When a gong is struck in a temple, it continues to sound long after the actual strike. If we are fascinated by a suiseki or a bonsai, and we cannot forget the experience, then we call this impression *yoin*.

In this case, we speak of a strong impressive power.

yugen (Japanese)

Concept that is difficult to define. It includes the notions: dark, obscure, mysterious, uncertain, profound, subtle. It is a subjective picture, for example, the moon shining behind a veil of clouds or a mountain hidden by the morning mist.

Notions and Features of Suiseki

balance

Aesthetically attractive, character, maturity, harmony and unity, proportions between different surfaces. Balance can refer to the vertical and horizontal, to light and dark, to straight and round, etc.

mineralogical features

Rock structure, compact mass, hardness (no visible occurrence of erosion over periods of time accessible to man); no crystals such as minerals.

rhythm

Lines, movement, tension, dramatics (dynamic outlines).

shape, form

Shaped only by nature, attractive shape, partial outlines such as triangles, circles, ovals. The only cut allowed is to create an even base.

suggestiveness

Expressive possibilities. Suggestiveness excites the human imagination and makes it discover images from a natural scene or an object of everyday life which corresponds to the shape of the stone. The more successful, the more valuable the suiseki (aesthetic standard).

surface, color

Surface structure, texture, color, color contrast between different parts, patina.

What to Look for when Buying a Suiseki

■■ The stone should not be damaged in any way.

■■ The base of the stone should be natural. When the base is too uneven, it may be cut, but this reduces the value of the stone.

■■ The stone must have no visible cracks.

■■ With a flat stone, you can perform a resonance test. Hang the stone on a thread or rope and tap it with a finger. If the stone has no cracks, you will hear a clear, pure tone. The pitch of the sound depends on the size of the stone. You can also use this resonance test for *suiban* and bonsai pots.

■■ A stone should not be oiled to enhance its colors.

■■ Check to see that the stone has not been lacquered (with a colorless lacquer).

■■ Check whether deep cracks in the stone have been filled in with white plastic simulating a mountain stream or a waterfall!

■■ Check whether parts of the stone have been glued together!

■■ A suiseki stone may not be carved or polished. It may, however, be cleaned.

■■ Check whether acid stains remain as a result of a cleaning process.

■■ Minerals, for example crystals, are not suiseki.

■■ A suiseki stone should be hard.

■■ Suiseki lovers appreciate dark (gray to black) colors, but brown, purple black, green black, and blue black are also interesting and impressive.

Suiseki Classification

Sizes for suiseki are given in centimeters in Japan, Korea, and Europe. In North America, inches are used (see Fig. 29).

The sequence of dimensions is width, depth, and height in Japan. In Korea, it is width, height, and depth.

Stylistic Classification of Suiseki

I. Shape
    A. Landscape stones (mountains, mountain ranges, etc.)
    B. Object stones (man, animal, house, etc.)

II. Surface patterns
    A. Human
    B. Animal
    C. Plant
    D. Landscape
    E. Celestial
    F. Weather
    G. Abstract

III. Place of origin

IV. Color

I. Shape
    A. Landscape stones
        1. Scenic landscape—
          sansui kei-seki, sansui keijo-seki

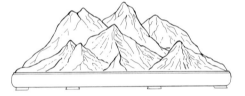

          a. Distant mountain—
          oyama-ishi, enzan-seki

          b. Near-view mountain—*kinzan-seki*

          c. Island mountain—one or several mountains standing on a flat stone plate; sugarloaf island mountain, when the elevation is high; shield island mountain, when the elevation is low

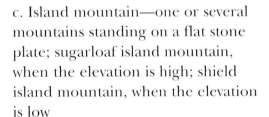

          d. Mountain with ice and snow or glacier

e. Mountain with lake

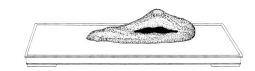

2. Mountain stream—*keiryu-seki*

3. Waterfall—*taki-ishi*
   a. Thread waterfall
   b. Sheet waterfall
   c. Dry waterfall

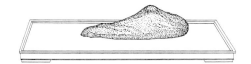

4. Plateau—*dan-seki or dan-ishi*

5. Slope—*doha-seki*

6. Shore—*isogata-ishi*
   a. Reef—*araiso-seki*

   b. Sandbar—*hirasu-ishi*

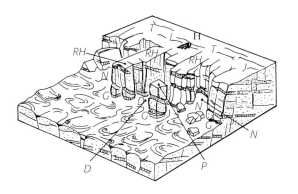

7. Coastal rock—*iwagata-ishi*

   a. Cliff areas with reef horn   RH
   b. Cliff areas with reef pillar   P
   c. Cliff areas with reef door   D
   d. Cliff areas with reef niche   N
   e. Transverse breaks   T
   f. Lengthwise breaks   L
   g. Holes   H
   h. Reef gorges   G

8. Island—*shimagata-ishi*

9. Cave—*dokutsu-ishi*

10. Shelter—*yadori/aayadori-ishi*

11. Tunnel—*domon-ishi*

12. Water pool—*mizutamari-ishi*

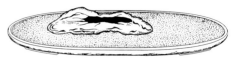

13. Karstic
  a. Groove karren

  b. Hollow karren

  c. Flat karren   F
     Pointed karren   S
     Fissure   K
     Layer joint   SV

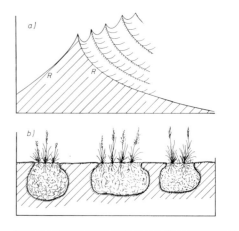

  d. Stalactites, stalagmites, and sinter "curtain" stones

14. Typical erosion mountain, as found in Monument Valley

15. Canyon shape

B. Object stones—*keisho-ishi*
   1. Human shapes—*sugata-ishi/jim butsu-seki*

   2. Animal shapes—*dobutsu-seki*
      a. Fish—*uogata-ishi*

      b. Bird—*torigata-ishi*

      c. Insect—*mushigata-ishi*

      d. Mammal (dog, horse, ox, bear, etc.)

   3. House shapes—*yagata-ishi*

   4. Bridge shapes—*hashi-ishi*

5. Boat shapes—*funagata-ishi*

6. Abstract shapes

II. Stones with extraordinary surface patterns

A. Human patterns

B. Animal patterns

C. Plant patterns

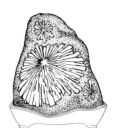

1. Chrysanthemum—*kikka-seki*

2. Japanese plum blossom—*baika-seki*

3. Leaf—*hagata-ishi*

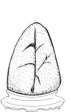

4. Grass—*kusagata-ishi*

5. Fruit—*migata-ishi*

D. Landscape patterns

E. Celestial patterns—*gensho-seki*

1. Moon—*tsukigata-ishi*

2. Sun—*higata-ishi*

3. Star—*hoshigata-ishi*

F. Weather patterns—*tenko-seki*

1. Rain—*amagata-ishi*

2. Snow—*yukigata-ishi*

3. Lightning—*raiko-seki*

G. Abstract patterns—*chusho-seki*

1. Snake—*jagure*

2. Pit mark—*sudachi*

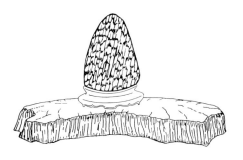

3. Tangled net—*itomaki-ishi*

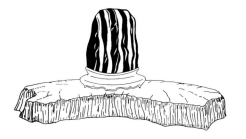

4. Tiger stripe—*tora-ishi*

III. Classification of suiseki by place of origin
   A. Place of origin
   B. Area, region
   C. Country

IV. Classification of suiseki by color
   A. Jet black—*maguro-ishi*
   B. Grey to black—*kuro-ishi*
   C. Red—*aka-ishi*
   D. Purple—*murasaki-ishi*
   E. Blue—*ao-ishi*
   F. Yellow red—*kinko-seki*
   G. Golden yellow—*ogon-ishi*
   H. Five color—*goshiki-ishi/goshiki-seki*

Recipes for Treating Wood

Polishing preparation for mat or wood

Mix together one part vinegar, one part pure alcohol, and one part turpentine oil. Add linseed oil to the mixture and stir thoroughly. Use a piece of cloth to apply small quantities of the preparation in circles on the surface. Keep the preparation in a cool place in a closed bottle.

Polishing oil for soft wood

Heat one part linseed oil. Add one part turpentine oil to the hot linseed oil and mix thoroughly. Apply the hot mixture with a soft cloth to a clean wood surface.

Wax polishing

Recipe 1
Melt 2 ounces beeswax in a boiler. Crumble 1½ ounces resin in a mortar and add slowly to the melting wax. Mix carefully and let cool. Apply light coats on the wood with a soft cloth or a brush.

Recipe 2
Melt I ounce carnauba wax and 1 ounce beeswax in a boiler. Add 7 ounces turpentine oil to the liquid and stir vigorously until the mixture thickens. When cold, apply light coats with a wool cloth. Brush the polished wood.

Index